EveryDay Spanish

EveryDay
Spanish

—⁓—

LOURDES ALCAÑIZ

MADISON
PARK
PRESS™

NEW YORK

Published by Madison Park Press, 15 East 26th Street, New York, NY 10010. Madison Park Press is a trade-
mark of Bookspan.

Book design by Christos Peterson

ISBN: 978-1-58288-278-9

Printed in the United States of America

Contents

—m—

Introduction

—ϻ—

Learning a new language is a long and sometimes difficult process. You may just want to exchange a few sentences with a Spanish-speaker or you may be a student looking to improve your Spanish vocabulary. In any case, this book is made for you. Listing the most useful words in Spanish, this manual will help you communicate with Spanish-speaking people and extend your vocabulary. You can look up a word in English or in Spanish as lists are alphabetically ordered in both languages. Some words have different names depending on the country; you will find the other name in parentheses.

In addition to the most common words, you will find vocabulary lists for the most common situations in your day-to-day life. Below these lists are some everyday actions that relate to the day-to-day situations as well as a few useful sentences that can be used in those instances. At the end of the book you will find more lists on subjects such as how to say the time, numbers, colors, and even food.

When there is a need to communicate in a foreign language we often find ourselves at a loss for words. Not anymore with this book!

Just a Few Basic Rules

—ᘏᘏ—

Nouns

Nouns are the words we use to name objects, animals, and people. In Spanish, unlike English, these words have gender and number, that is, they could be masculine or feminine as well as singular or plural.

- MASCULINE/FEMININE: In general, masculine names end in "o" or "on" and feminine names in "a," but there are exceptions. Examples of masculine names are: *niño* (boy), *ladrillo* (brick), and *camión* (truck). Examples of feminine names include: *niña* (girl), *casa* (house), and *pelota* (ball).

- SINGULAR/PLURAL: To make a word plural you add "s" if it ends in a vowel and "es" if the ending is a consonant. For example: *casa(s)* or *camion(es)*.

Articles

Articles are those short little words that go before the names of objects, animals, or people we are referring to (i.e., *the* house). In Spanish the article's gender (masculine/feminine) and number (singular/plural) have to coincide with the name that follows. The masculine article is *el* and the feminine *la*, but there are other types of articles. The plural of *el* is *los* and the plural of *la* is *las*. Therefore we would say: *la casa* (the house), *las casas* (the houses), *el camión* (the truck), *los camiones* (the trucks).

Verbs

These words indicate the action being performed by the person, animal, or object we are talking about, for example: *el niño corre* (the boy runs). In Spanish, words ending in "ar," "er," or "ir" are usually verbs. This way of writing the verb is called *infinitive* and it corresponds with the form *to* (run, for example) in English.

As in English, Spanish verbs are conjugated: they change depending on who is performing them (*yo, tú, el;* I, you, he/she), but don't worry, you can be understood without knowing all the possible conjugations.

Other Words

There are other words that complete sentences as adjectives or adverbs.

- ADJECTIVES tell us qualities about the person, animal, or object we are referring to. For example: *La casa es verde* (The house is green). In Spanish, contrary to English, adjectives go after the noun. For instance, in Spanish we would say: *Un auto grande,* while in English we would say: A big car.

- ADVERBS tell us how an action is being performed: *Pepe salta alegremente* (Pepe jumps happily). In English, when these adverbs refer to how the action is being performed, they end in "ly" (quickly, easily). In Spanish they end in "mente": *rápidamente, fácilmente.*

  Adverbs also refer to when (*Ayer fui al cine*/Yesterday I went to the cinema) and where (*Yo vivo aquí*/I live here) the action is performed.

- CONJUNCTIONS link words and sentences, as in this example using the conjunction "y" (and): *María y Juan van de compras* (María and Juan are going shopping).

Sentence Word Order

In Spanish, as in English, it is difficult to be understood if the words of a sentence are not placed in the right order. The simplest and most efficient way to communicate in Spanish is with the following sentence structure: article + noun + verb + other words (adverbs, names, adjectives, etc). This way of ordering a sentence is also known as subject + verb + object: *La niña es guapa* (The girl is pretty).

EveryDay Spanish

The Most Useful Spanish Words
Spanish-to-English Alphabetical List

a	to
abajo	down
abdomen	abdomen
abeja	bee
abierto	open
abogado	lawyer
abrazar	to embrace
abrazo	hug
abrigo	coat
abril	April
abuela	grandmother
abuelo	grandfather
acabar	to finish
acceso	access
acción	action
aceite	oil
aceite de oliva	olive oil
acelga	Swiss chard
aceptar	accept
acerca	about

ácido	acid
aclarar	to clarify
acompañar	to accompany
aconsejar	to advise
acostarse	go to bed
acto	act
actual	current
acuarela	water colors
acuerdo	agreement
adelante	forward, ahead
además	moreover
adiós	good-bye
adjuntar	to attach
aduana	custom
afectuoso	affectionate
agente	agent
agosto	August
agradecer	to thank
agua	water
agua caliente	hot water
agua fría	cold water
aguacate (also *palta*)	avocado
águila	eagle
aguja	needle
agujero	hole
ahora	now
aire	air

ajo	garlic
ajuste	adjustment
alambre	wire
a la plancha	grilled
albaricoque	apricot
albóndigas	meatballs
alcachofa	artichoke
alcalde	mayor
alcoba (also *dormitorio*)	bedroom
alergia	allergy
alfombra	rug
alfombrilla	mat
alfombrilla de hule	rubber mat
algodón	cotton
alguien	someone
alguno	some
aliento	breath
alisado con secador	blow dry
al lado	beside
allí	there
almacén	department store
almeja	clam
almohada	pillow, cushion
almorzar	to have lunch
alquilar	to rent
altavoz	loudspeaker
alto	tall

altura	height
alumno	student
amargo	bitter
amarillo	yellow
ambos	both
amigo	friend
amistad	friendship
amor	love
añadir	to add
analgésico	pain reliever
anaranjado	orange
ancho	wide
anestesia	anesthesia
ángulo	angle
anillo	ring
animal	animal
anoche	last night
antebrazo	forearm
antes	before
antiácido	antacid
antihistamínico	antihistamine
antitérmico	fever reducer
anuncio	advertisement, announcement
aparato	machine, appliance, apparatus
aparcar (also *estacionar*)	to park

aparecer	to appear
apartamento	apartment
apellido	surname
apio	celery
aplastar	to crush
apoyar	to support
aprendizaje	learning
apresurarse	to hurry
aprobación	approval
aprovecharse	to take advantage of
aproximación	approach
aquel	that
aquella	that
aquellos	those
aquí	here
arado	plough
araña	spider
arbeja (also *guisante*)	pea
árbol	tree
archivador	filing cabinet
arco	arch
ardilla	squirrel
arena	sand
arete	earring
armario	closet, locker
armonía	harmony

arquitecto	architect
arrastrar	drag
arreglar	to fix
arriba	up
arroz	rice
arruga	wrinkle
arte	art
artículo	article
artista	artist
asado	roasted, barbecued
asco	disgust
asegurar	to insure
así	thus
asiento	seat
asiento de automóvil	car seat
áspero	rough
aspiradora	vacuum cleaner
asunto	matter
ataque	attack
atención	attention
atizador	poker
atornillar	to screw
atracción	attraction
atrás	back, behind
a través	across
atreverse	to dare
aunque	although

auriculares	headphones
autobús	bus
automático	automatic
automóvil	automobile
autopista (also *carretera*)	highway
autoridad	authority
ave	fowl
avena	oats
avenida	avenue
avión	airplane
avispa	wasp
ayer	yesterday
ayuda	help
ayudar	to help
ayuntamiento	town hall
azafata	flight attendant
azúcar	sugar
azul	blue
azul marino	navy blue
bailar	to dance
baile	dance
bajar	to go down
bajo	short
balanza	scale
balcón	balcony
ballena	whale
bañar	to bathe

banco	bench
banda	band
bandeja	tray
bandera	flag
bañera	bathtub
baño	bath
baranda	handrail
barato	cheap
barba	beard
barbilla	chin
barco	boat
barra	rod
barrio (also *vecindario*)	neighborhood
báscula	scale
base	base
base de datos	database
bastante	enough
basura	garbage
batidora	blender
bebé	baby
beber	to drink
bebida	drink
bella, bello	beautiful
beneficio	profit, benefit
berenjena	eggplant
berro	watercress
besar	to kiss

beso	kiss
biberón	baby bottle
biblioteca	library
bicicleta	bicycle
bidé	bidet
bienvenida	welcome
blanco	white
blusa	blouse
boca	mouth
bocina	horn
bocinas	speakers
boda	wedding
boleto	ticket
bolígrafo	ballpoint pen
bolsa	bag
bolsillo	pocket
bombear	to pump
bombilla	lightbulb
bonito	pretty
borde	edge
borracho	drunk
bosque	forest
bota	boot
botella	bottle
botiquín	medicine chest
botón	button
brasier (also *sostén*)	bra

brazo	arm
brécol (also *brócoli*)	broccoli
brillante	bright
broma	joke
brotes de soya	soy sprouts
bueno	good
bulbo	bulb
bulto	bump
burro	donkey
búsqueda	search
caballo	horse
cabello	hair
cabeza	head
cable	cord
cabra	goat
cacahuate (also *maní*)	peanut
cada	every, each
cadena	chain
cadera	hip
caer	to fall
cafetera	coffee pot
caída	fall
caja	box
caja	cashier
cajero	cashier
cajón	drawer
calabacín (also *calabacita*)	zucchini

calabaza	pumpkin
calcetín (also media)	sock
calidad	quality
caliente	warm
callado	quiet
calle	street
calor	heat
cama	bed
cama de matrimonio	double bed
cama individual	single bed
cámara	camera
camarero	waiter
camarón	shrimp
cambiar	to change
cambio	exchange
caminar	to walk
camino	road
camión	truck
camisa	shirt
camiseta	T-shirt
camisón	nightdress
camote	sweet potato
campana	bell
campo	field
canario	canary
canción	song
canela	cinnamon

cansado	tired
cantar	to sing
caoba	auburn
capaz	able
carbón	coal
cárcel	jail
cargar	to charge
carne	meat
carnicería	butcher's shop
caro	expensive
carpeta	folder
carpintero	carpenter
carretera	road
carretilla	wheelbarrow
carrito	shopping cart
carro	cart, car
carta	letter
carta (also *menú*)	menu
casa	house
casado	married
casi	almost
castaño	chestnut
castigo	punishment
castillo	castle
causar	to cause
cebolla	onion
ceja	eyebrow

celeste	sky blue
cenicero	ashtray
centígrado	centigrade
centímetro	centimeter
centrifugado	spin-dry
centro	center
centro comercial	mall
cepillo	brush
cepillo de dientes	toothbrush
cera	wax
ceras	crayons
cerca	near, close
cerdo	pig, pork
cereal	cereal
cerebro	brain
cereza	cherry
cerilla (also *fósforo*)	match
cerrojo	lock
certificado	certified
cerumen	earwax
cesta	basket
champiñones (also *hongos*)	mushrooms
champú	shampoo
change	cambio
chaqueta	jacket
cheque	check
chimenea	chimney

chincheta (also *tachuela*)	thumbtack
chiste	joke
chocar	to crash
chófer	driver
chupón	pacifier
ciclo	cycle
ciego	blind
cielo	sky
ciencia	science
cierto	certain
cine	movie theater
cinta adhesiva	adhesive tape
cinta para correr	treadmill
cintura	waist
cinturón	belt
cinturón de seguridad	seat belt
círculo	circle
ciruela	plum
cita	appointment
ciudad	city
ciudadano	citizen
clase	classroom
clavo	nail
cliente	client
clima	climate
clip	clip
cloro	bleach

cobija	blanket
cobre	copper
cobro	charge
cocido (also *hervido*)	boiled
cocina	kitchen
cocinado	cooked
cocinar	to cook
cocinero	cook
codo	elbow
coincidencia	coincidence
col (also *repollo*)	cabbage
cola	tail
colcha	bedspread
colchón	mattress
coles de Bruselas	Brussels sprouts
coliflor	cauliflower
colirio	eye drops
collar	necklace
colonia	cologne
color	color
combustible	fuel
comedor	dining room
comenzar	to begin
comer	to eat
comezón (also *picazón*)	itching
comida	meal, food
comida para bebé	baby food

comité	committee
como	like, as
comodidad	comfort
cómodo	comfortable
compañía	company
comparación	comparison
competencia (also *concurso*)	competition
complejo	complex
complementos (also *accesorios*)	accessories
completer	to complete
completo	complete
comportamiento	behavior
comprar	to buy, to shop
comprender	to understand
compresas	sanitary napkins
compromiso	engagement
computadora	computer
común	common
condición	condition
conejo	rabbit
conexión	connection
conferencia	conference
confiar	to trust
confundido	confused
congelado	frozen
congelador	freezer
conocer	to know

conocimiento	knowledge
consciente	conscious
consulado	consulate
contable (also *contador*)	accountant
contar	to count
contraseña (also *clave*)	password
continuar	to continue
contra	against
control	control
control remoto	remote control
copa	cup
copa de vino	wine glass
copia	copy
copiar	to copy
corazón	heart
corazón de palmito	hearts of palm
corbata	tie
corcho	cork
cordel (also *cuerda*)	string
cordero	lamb
correcto	correct
correo	mail
correo electrónico	e-mail
correr	to run
cortar	to cut
corte	cut
cortés	polite

cortina	curtain
cortina de baño	shower curtain
corto	short
cosas de aseo	toiletries
coser	to sew
costa	coast
costumbre	custom
crecer	to grow
crédito	credit
creencia	belief
creer	to believe
crema	cream
crema agria	sour cream
crema de belleza	beauty cream
crema hidratante	moisturizing cream
crema para picaduras	cream for insect bites
cremallera (also *cierre*)	zipper
crimen	crime
cristal	glass
crudo	raw
cruel	cruel
cruz	cross
cruzar	to cross
cuaderno	notebook
cuadra	block
cuadro	painting, picture
cualquiera	any

cuando	when
cuarto	room
cuarto de baño	restroom, bathroom
cubitos de hielo	ice cubes
cubo (also *balde*)	bucket
cubrir	to cover
cuchara	spoon
cucharada	tablespoon
cucharita de café	coffee spoon
cucharita de té	teaspoon
cucharón	ladle
cuchilla	blade
cuchillo	knife
cuello	neck
cuenta	account, bill
cuenta corriente	checking account
cuenta de ahorros	savings account
cuento	story, tale
cuerdo	sane
cuero	leather
cuerpo	body
cuervo	crow
cuidar	to take care
cumpleaños	birthday
cuna	crib
cuñada	sister-in-law
cuñado	brother-in-law

cura	priest
curso	course
curva	curve
dama	lady
dañar	to damage
dar	to give
de	from, of
de nuevo	again
debajo	under
débil	feeble, weak
decidir	to decide
decir	to say
decir adiós	to say good-bye
decisión	decision
dedo	finger
dedos de los pies	toes
dejar	to leave, to let be
delante	in front of
delfín	dolphin
delgado	thin
delicado	delicate
demasiado	too much
dentista	dentist
dentro	inside
dependiente	dependent
depilación	depilation
deporte	sport

depósito	deposit, tank
derecha	right
derecho	straight
desagüe	drain
desarrollar	to develop
desarrollo	development
desayuno	breakfast
descansar	to rest
descargar	download
descubrimiento	discovery
descubrir	to discover
desear	to desire
deseo	desire
desgracia	misfortune
desodorante	deodorant
despacio	slowly
despensa	pantry
despertarse	to wake up
despierto	awake
después	after
destapador	bottle opener
destinatario	addressee
destino	destination
destornillador	screwdriver
destrucción	destruction
detalle	detail
detergente	detergent

detrás	behind
deuda	debt
día	day
diarrea	diarrhea
dibujo	drawing
diciembre	December
diente	tooth
diferente	different
dificultad	difficult
digestión	digestion
dinero	money
dinero en efectivo	cash
dios	god
dirección	address, direction
discusión	argument, discussion
diseño	design
disfrutar	to enjoy, to have a good time
distancia	distance
distribución	distribution
diversión	amusement
división	division
doblado	bent
doblar	to fold
docena	dozen
dólar	dollar
dolor	pain

dolor de garganta	sore throat
domingo	Sunday
dónde	where
dormir	to sleep
ducha	shower
ducharse	to shower
dudar	to doubt
dueño	owner
dulce	sweet
durar	to last
durazno	peach
duro	hard
economista	economist
edad	age
edificio	building
edredón	comforter
educación	education
efecto	effect
ejemplo	example
ejército	army
ejotes (also *judías verdes*)	green beans
él	he
el, la, los, las	the
elástico	elastic
electricista	electrician
elefante	elefant
elevador	elevator

elevar	to lift
ella	she
ellas, ellos	they
empleado	employee
empleo	employment
empresario	businessman
empujar	to push
en	at, on, in
enamorado	in love
encantado	delighted
encima	over, above
encontrar	to find
endivias	endives
enero	January
enfermedad	disease
enfermo	ill, sick
engañar	to deceive
enjuagar	to rinse
enjuague bucal	mouthwash
enlace	link
enojado	angry
enojar	to annoy
enseñar	to teach, to show
entonces	then
entrada	entrance
entrar	to enter
entre	among, between

entregar	to deliver
entrenador	trainer
entumecimiento	numbness
envase	container
enviar	to send
envío	shipment
envolver	to wrap
equilibrio	balance
equipaje	luggage
equipo	team
equipo de música	music equipment, stereo
error	error
eructar	burp
escalera	staircase
escalera mecánica	escalator
escalofrío	chill
escalón	step
escaparate	shop window
escoba	broom
escobilla del inodoro	toilet brush
escoger	to choose
esconder	to hide
escribir	to write
escucha	listen
escuchar	to listen, to hear
escuela	school

esfuerzo	effort
esguince	sprain
espacio	space
espalda	back
español	Spanish
espárragos	asparagus
espátula	spatula
espejo	mirror
espejo retrovisor	rear mirror
esperanza	hope
esperar	to wait, to hope
espinaca	spinach
esponja	sponge
espuma	foam, lather
espumadera	skimmer
esqueleto	skeleton
esquina	corner
estación	station, season
estante	shelf
estantería	shelves
estar	to be
estatua	statue
este	east
estirar	pull
estómago	stomach
estornudo	sneeze
estrecho	narrow

estrella	star
estudiante	student
estudiar	to study
estufa	heater
evento	event
examen	exam
exigir	to demand
existencia	existence
éxito	success
expansión	expansion
experiencia	experience
experimento	experiment
experto	expert
explicar	to explain
explotar	to explode
extrañar	to miss
extraño	strange
fábrica	factory
fácil	easy
factura	bill
falda	skirt
fallar	to fail
falso	false
familia	family
famoso	famous
fantástico	fantastic, great
farmacia	pharmacy

fax	fax
fe	faith
febrero	February
fecha	date
felicidades	congratulations
feliz	happy
feo	ugly
ferrocarril	railroad
fértil	fertile
fertilizante	fertilizer
ficción	fiction
fiebre	fever
fiesta	party
fijo	fixed
filtro solar	sunscreen
fin	end
firma	signature
firmar	to sign
físico	physical
flequillo	bangs
flor	flower
florero	vase
fontanero	plumber
forma	form
fórmula	formula
formularios	forms
fósforo	match

foto	photo
fotocopia	photocopy
fotocopiadora	photocopier
frambuesa	raspberry
francés	French
frase	phrase, sentence
frecuente	frequent
freno	brake
frente	front, forehead
fresa	strawberry
fresco	fresh
frijoles	beans
frío	cold
frito	fried
frontera	border
frotar	rub
fruta	fruit
fucsia	fuchsia
fuego	fire
fuera	outside
fuerte	strong
fuerza	force
fumador	smoker
fumar	to smoke
funda de almohada	pillowcase
fútbol	soccer
futuro	future

gafas	eyeglasses
galletas	cookies
galletitas saladas	crackers
gallina	hen
ganar	to earn
gancho	hook
ganglio	node
garbanzos	chickpeas
garganta	throat
gasoil	diesel
gasolina	gasoline
gastar	to spend, to waste
gato	cat
gelatina	jelly, gelatin
general	general
gente	people
gerente	manager
gimnasia	gymnastics
gobierno	government
golpe	blow
gordo	fat
gorrión	sparrow
gota	drop
gracias	thanks
grado	degree
gramo	gram
granate	maroon

grande	big
granja	farm
grano	grain
grapadora	stapler
gratis	free
grieta	crack
grifo (also *llave*)	faucet
gris	grey
gritar	to shout
grito	shout
grúa	crane
grupo	group
guante	glove
guantera	glove compartment
guantes	gloves
guapo	handsome
guardar	save
guardia	guard
guía	guide
guisante (also *arbeja*)	pea
habitación	room
habitación doble	double room
habitación simple	single room
hablar	to speak
hacer	to do, to make
hacer el amor	to make love
hacia	toward

hambre	hunger
hasta	until
hay	there is
hecho	fact
helado	ice cream
hembra	female
herida	injury
hermana	sister
hermano	brother
hervidor	kettle
hervir	boiling
hielo	ice
hierba (also *pasto*)	grass
hierro	iron
hígado	liver
hija	daughter
hijo	son
hilo dental	dental floss
hinchazón	swelling
hipoteca	mortgage
historia	history
hoja	leaf
hola	hello
hombre	man
hombro	shoulder
hongos (also *champiñones*)	mushrooms
hora	hour

horario	schedule
hormiga	ant
hornillo	ring, portable stove
horno	oven
hospital	hospital
hoy	today
hueco	hollow
huelga	strike
hueso	bone
hueso roto	broken bone
huesped	guest
huevo	egg
humo	smoke
humor	humor
idea	idea
idioma	language
iglesia	church
igual	equal
impermeable	raincoat
importante	important
imprimir	print
imprudente	foolish
impuesto	tax
impulso	impulse
incluso	even
incrementar	increase
indicador	indicator

índice	rate
industria	industry
infección	infection
inflamación	inflammation
ingeniero	engineer
inglés	English
inmediatamente	immediately
inodoro	toilet
insecto	insect
insensibilidad	numbness
insertar	to insert
instrumento	instrument
intentar	to try
intento	attempt
interés	interest
intermitente	indicator
Internet	Internet
intervalo	interval
inútil	useless
invención	invention
invierno	winter
ir	to go
irritación	irritation
isla	island
izquierda	left
jabón	soap
jabón lavavajillas	dishwasher soap

jamón	ham
jarabe para la tos	cough syrup
jardín	garden
jarra	mug
jefe	boss, chief
jilguero	goldfinch
jirafa	giraffe
joven	young
joya	jewel
joyería	jewelry store
judías verdes (also *ejotes*)	green beans
juego	game
jueves	Thursday
juez	judge
jugar	to play
jugo de naranja	orange juice
juguete	toy
julio	July
junio	June
juntos	together
jurar	to swear
kilo	kilo
kilómetro	kilometer
kiwi	kiwi
la, el, los, las	the
labios	lips
lado	side

ladrillo	brick
ladrón	thief
lago	lake
lamentar	to regret
lámpara	lamp
lana	wool
lanzar	to throw
lápices de colores	colored pencils
lápiz	pencil
largo	long
lata	can
latón	brass
lavabo	sink
lavadora	washing machine
lavaplatos	dishwasher
lavar	to wash
lavar a mano	hand wash
laxante	laxative
lección	lesson
leche	milk
lechuga	lettuce
lector de DVD	DVD player
lectura	reading
leer	to read
lejos	far
leña	wood
lengua	tongue

lenguado	sole fish
lenguaje	language
lentamente	slowly
lentejas	lentils
león	lion
lesión	injury
levantarse	to get up
ley	law
libre	free
librería	bookstore
libro	book
licor	liquor
lienzo	canvas
lima	file
límite	limit
limpiador de cristales	glass cleaner
limpiador de grasa	grease cleaner
limpiador de suelos	floor cleaner
limpiaparabrisas	windshield wipers
limpiar	to clean
limpieza de cutis	facial
limpieza en seco	dry cleaning
limpio	clean
línea	line
lino	linen
líquido	liquid
lista	list

listo	ready, smart
llama	flame
llamada	call
llamar	to call
llave	key, faucet
llave inglesa	wrench
llegada	arrival
llegar	to arrive
llenar	to fill
lleno	full
llevar	to carry
llorar	to cry
llover	to rain
lluvia	rain
lobo	wolf
loco	crazy
los, el, la, las	the
lucha	fight
luego	after
lugar	place
lujo	luxury
luna	moon
lunes	Monday
luz	light
madera	wood
madre	mother
maduro	ripe

maestro	teacher
maíz (also *elote*)	corn
mala hierba	weed
maleta	suitcase
malo	bad
mamadera	baby bottle
mamila	baby-bottle nipple
mañana	morning, tomorrow
mancha	stain
mandarina	tangerine
mandíbula	jaw
manejar	driving
manga de riego (also *manguera*)	hose
mango	mango
manicura	manicure
mano	hand
manta	blanket
mantel	tablecloth
mantener	to keep
mantequilla	butter
manzana	apple
mapa	map
máquina	machine
máquina de café	coffee machine
máquina de cortar pasto	lawn mower
maquinilla de afeitar	shaver

mar	sea
marca	mark
marco	frame
mareo	dizziness
margarina	margarine
margarita	daisy
marisco	shellfish
marrón	brown
martes	Tuesday
martillo	hammer
marzo	March
más	more
matemáticas	math
material	material
matrimonio	marriage
mayo	May
mayonesa	mayonnaise
media	stocking, sock
medianoche	midnight
medicina	medicine, drug
médico	physician, doctor
medida	measure
medio	middle
mediodía	noon
mejilla	cheek
mejillón	mussel
mejor	better

mejorar	to improve
melocotón (also durazno)	peach
melón	melon
memoria	memory
menos	less
mente	mind
mentira	lie
menú	menu
mercado	market
merecer	to deserve
merienda	snack
merluza	hake
mes	month
mesa	table, desk
mesa de café	coffee table
mesa de comer	dining table
mesa de estudio	study desk
mesero	waiter
mesita de noche	nightstand
metal	metal
metálico	metallic
método	method
metro	meter
mezclado	mixed
mi, mis	my
microondas	microwave
miedo	fear

miembro	member
mientras	while
miércoles	Wednesday
milagro	miracle
milímetro	millimeter
militar	military
milla	mile
mina	mine
minuto	minute
mío	mine
mirar	to look
mirilla	peephole
misa	mass
mismo	same
mitad	half
moda	fashion
moisés	bassinet
mojar	to wet
molestar	to bother
moneda	coin
mono	monkey
montaña	mountain
morena, moreno	brunette, brunet
moretón	bruise
morir	to die
mortadela	bologna
mosca	fly

mosquitera	mosquito net
mosquito	mosquito
mostrar	to show
motor	engine
mover	to move
movimiento	motion, move
muchacha	girl
muchacho	boy
mucho	a lot of, much, very
muebles	furniture
muerte	death
muerto	dead
muestra	sample
mujer	woman
mundo	world
muñeca	doll, wrist
músculo	muscles
museo	museum
música	music
muslo	thigh
muy hecho	overdone
nabo	turnip
nacer	to be born
nacimiento	birth
nación	nation
nada	nothing
nadar	to swim

nadie	nobody
ñame	yam
naranja	orange
nariz	nose
natural	natural
náusea	nausea
navegador	browser
navegar	to sail, to navigate
Navidad	Christmas
neblina	mist
necesario	necessary
necesidad	need
necesitar	to need
nectarina	nectarine
negar	to deny
negocio	business
negro	black
nervio	nerve
nevar	to snow
ni	neither
niebla	fog
nieta	granddaughter
nieto	grandson
nieve	snow
niña	girl
ninguno	none
niño	boy

niño	child
níspero	medlar tree
nivel	level
no	no, not
no fumador	nonsmoker
noche	night
nombre	name
nombre de usuario	user name
normal	normal, regular
norte	north
nosotros	we
nota	note
noticia	news
novia	girlfriend
noviembre	November
novio	boyfriend
nube	cloud
nublado	cloudy
nudo	knot
nueces	nuts
nuera	daughter-in-law
nuestro	our
nuevo	new
número	number
nunca	never
o	or
objeto	object

obligar	to oblige
observación	observation
obtener	to get, to obtain
océano	ocean
octubre	October
ocupado	busy
ocurrir	to happen
odiar	to hate
oeste	west
oficina	office
ofrecer	to offer
oído	ear
ojo	eye
oler	to smell
olla	pot
olor	odor
onza	ounce
operación	operation
opinión	opinion
oportunidad	opportunity, chance
opuesto	opposite
orden	order
ordenar	order
orégano	oregano
oreja	ear
organización	organization
ornamento	ornament

oro	gold
oscuro	dark
osito	teddy bear
oso	bear
otoño	fall
otro	other
oveja	sheep
padre	father
pagar	to pay
página	page
página principal	homepage
página Web	Web page
pago	payment
país	country
paisaje	landscape
pájaro	bird
pala	shovel
palabra	word
palacio	palace
pálido	pale
palitos de algodón	cotton tips
paloma	pigeon
pan	bread
pan blanco	white bread
pan integral	whole wheat bread
panadería	bakery
panadero	baker

pañal	diaper
paño	cloth, duster
pantalla	display, screen
pantalones	pants
pantalones cortos	shorts
pantorrilla	calf
pañuelo	handkerchief
papa	potato
papaya	papaya
papel	paper
papel para regalo	wrapping paper
papelera	wastepaper basket
paquete	parcel, package
par	pair
para	for
parabrisas	windshield
paraguas	umbrella
paragüero	umbrella stand
paralelo	parallel
parar	to stop
parecer	to seem
pared	wall
pariente	relative
párpado	eyelid
parque	park
parquecito infantil	playpen
párrafo	paragraph

parte	part
pasa	raisin
pasado	past
pasajero	passenger
pasaporte	passport
pasar	to pass
paseo	stroll
pasillo	aisle
paso	step
pasta	pasta, paste
pastel	cake
pasto	grass
patada	kick
patillas	sideburns
patrón	boss
pavo	turkey
paz	peace
peatón	pedestrian
peca	freckle
pecado	sin
pecho	chest, breast
pedicura	pedicure
pegar	to hit
peine	comb
película	movie
peligro	danger
peligroso	dangerous

pelirrojo	red-haired, redhead
pelota	ball
pena	pity, grief
pensar	to think
peor	worse
pepino	cucumber
pequeño	little, small
percha	hanger
perchero	clothes rack
perder	to lose
pérdida	loss
perdón	pardon
perforadora	hole punch
perfume	perfume
perfumería	perfumery
periódico	newspaper
periodista	journalist
permanecer	to remain
permanente	perm, permanent
permiso	permission
permitir	to permit
pero	but
perro	dog
persona	person
pertenecer	to belong
pesado	heavy
pesar	to weigh

pesas	weights
pescadería	fishmonger's shop
pescado	fish
peso	weight
pestañas	eyelashes
petunia	petunia
pez	fish
picazón	itching
pico	pick
picoso (also *picante*)	spicy
pie	foot
piedra	stone
piel	skin
piernas	leg
pieza	piece
pijamas	pajamas
pila	sink, battery
píldora	pill
pileta	sink
pimienta	pepper (spice)
pimiento verde	green pepper
piña	pineapple
pintar	to paint
pintura	paint, painting
pinzas	clothes peg
pis	pee
piscina (also *alberca*)	swimming pool

piso	floor
pistola	gun
pizarra	blackboard
placer	pleasure
plancha	iron
planchar	to iron
planta	plant
plástico	plastic
plastilina	plasticine
plata	silver
plátano	plantain
plato	dish, plate
playa	beach
plaza	plaza
pliegue	fold
plomo	lead
pluma	feather, pen
plumero	feather duster
pobre	poor
poco	not much, little
poco hecho	raw
poder	power
poesía	poetry
policía	police
político	political, politician
pollo	chicken
polvo	dust, powder

poner	to put
por	by
por favor	please
por qué	why
porque	because
posible	possible
posición	position
postal	postcard
precio	price
pregunta	question
preguntar	to ask
preocuparse	to worry
preparar	to prepare
presente	present
préstamo	loan
prestar	to lend
presupuesto	budget
prima	female cousin
primavera	spring
primero	first
primo	male cousin
prisa	hurry
prisión	prison
privado	private
probable	probable
probador	fitting room
probar	to taste

problema	problem
proceso	process
producir	to produce
profesor	professor
profundo	deep
prohibir	to forbid
proyecto	project
promesa	promise
prometer	to promise
pronto	soon
propiedad	property
propietario	owner
propina	tip
propósito	purpose
prosa	prose
protector de labios	lip protector
proteger	to protect
protestar	to protest
provisiones	groceries
prueba	proof, test
público	public
pueblo	village
puede	may
puente	bridge
puerta	door
puerto	port, harbor
puesta de sol	sunset

pulgada	inch
pulgar	thumb
pulir	to polish
pulmón	lung
pulsera	bracelet
puño	fist
punto	point
puntos	stitches
pupilas	pupils
pupitre	desk
puré de papas	mashed potatoes
pus	pus
queja	complaint
quejarse	to complain
quemadura	burn
quemar	to burn
querer	to want, to love
querido	dear
queso	cheese
queso rallado	grated cheese
químico	chemical
quitagrapas	staple remover
quitar	to take away
quizás	perhaps
radio	radio
raíl	rail
raíz	root

rallador	grater
rama	branch
rana	frog
rango	range
rápido	quick
rastrillo	rake
rata	rat
ratón	mouse
rayo	ray
razón	reason
reacción	reaction
recepción	reception desk
receta	recipe, prescription
rechazar	to reject
recibir	to receive
recibo	receipt, ticket
recipiente	container
recogedor	dustpan
recoger	to pick up
recompensa	reward
reconocer	to recognize
recordar	to remember
red	net, network
redondo	round
refrigerador	refrigerator
regadera	shower, watering can
regalo	gift, present

régimen	regime
registro	record
regla	rule
regresar	to return
regular	regular, normal
rehogado	stir-fried
reina	queen
reír	to laugh
relación	relationship
religión	religion
reloj	clock
reloj de alarma	alarm clock
remedio	remedy
remitente	sender
remolacha	beetroot
remolcar	to tow
remoto	remote
repetir	to repeat
reposapiés	footrest
representante	representative
reserva, reservación	reservation
reservar	to reserve
resfriado	cold
residente	resident
respetar	to respect
respirar	to breathe
responder	to answer

responsable	responsible
respuesta	answer
resto	rest
retiro	withdrawal
retraso	delay
retrato	portrait
reunión	meeting, reunion
revelar	to reveal, to develop film
revista	magazine
rey	king
riñon	kidney
río	river
ritmo	rhythm
rizos	curls
robar	to steal
rodar	to roll
rodilla	knee
rojo	red
romper	to break
roncar	to snore
ropa	clothes
ropa blanca	white clothes
ropa de color	colored clothes
ropa interior	underwear
rosado	pink
rostro	face

roto	broken
rotulador	marker
rubio	blond
rueda	tire
rueda de repuesto	spare tire
ruido	noise
ruidoso	loud
rulo	curler
ruta	route
sábado	Saturday
sábana	sheet
saber	to know
sacacorchos	corkscrew
sacar	to take out
sal	salt
sala de pesas	weight room
sala de reuniones	meeting room
saldo	balance
salida	exit
salir	to leave
salmón	salmon
salón	living room, classroom
salsa	sauce
saltar	to jump
salud	health
saludable	healthy

saludar	to greet
saludo	greeting
sandalias	sandals
sandía	watermelon
sangre	blood
sapo	toad
sardina	sardine
sartén	pan, frying pan
satisfecho	satisfied
sauna	sauna
secador de pelo	hairdryer
secadora	dryer
secar	to dry
sección	section
seco	dry
secreción	secretion
secretaria	secretary
secreto	secret
sed	thirst
seda	silk
seguir	to follow
según	according to
segundo	second
seguridad	security
seguro	safe, insurance
selección	selection
sello	stamp

semana	week
semilla	seed
señor	sir
señora	madam
sentarse	to sit down
sentimiento	feeling
separar	to separate
septiembre	September
ser	to be
serio	serious
serpiente	snake
servilleta	napkin
servir	to serve
sexo	sex
si	if
sí	yes
siempre	always
sierra	saw
siesta	nap
siglo	century
signature	firma
signo	sign
siguiente	next
silla	chair
simpático	nice, pleasant
simple	simple
sin	without

sirviente	servant
sitio	place
sobre	envelope
sobrina	niece
sobrino	nephew
sofá	couch
sol	sun
solamente	only
solicitar	to request
solo	alone
sombra	shade
sombrero	hat
sonreír	to smile
sonrisa	smile
sopera	soup tureen
suavizante	softener, conditioner
subir	to go up
súbitamente	suddenly
sucio	dirty
sudor	sweat
suegra	mother-in-law
suegro	father-in-law
sueño	sleep
suerte	luck
sueter	sweater
suficiente	enough
suma	addition

supermercado	supermarket
supurar	fester
sur	south
tabaco	tobacco
tabla	board
tabla de planchar	ironing board
taladradora	drill
talla	size
tallas grandes	plus sizes
tallas pequeñas	petite sizes
tamaño	size
también	also
tampoco	neither
tampón	tampon
tapón	plug
tarde	late, afternoon
tarea	work
tarjeta	card
tarjeta de crédito	credit card
taza	cup
tazón	bowl
teatro	theater
techo	ceiling, roof
teclado	keyboard
tela	cloth
teléfono	telephone
televisor	television

temperatura	temperature
temprano	early
tenazas	pliers
tendedero	clothesline
tendón	tendons
tenedor	fork
tenedor de trinchar	carving fork
tener	to have
tetera	teapot
tía	aunt
tiburón	shark
tiempo	time
tienda	shop
tierra	earth, land, soil
tigre	tiger
tijeras	scissors
timbre	doorbell
tina	bathtub
tinta	ink
tinte	dye
tío	uncle
típico	typical
tipo	kind
tipo de interés	interest rate
tirar	to throw
tiza	chalk
toalla	towel

toallas sanitarias (also *compresas*)	sanitary napkins
toallita de baño	washcloth
toallitas húmedas	baby wipes
tobillo	ankle
tocador	dressing table
tocar	to touch
todavía	still
todo	all, everything
todos	everybody
tomate	tomato
tonelada	ton
tormenta	storm
tornillo	screw
toro	bull
toronja (also *pomelo*)	grapefruit
torre	tower
tos	cough
toser	to cough
tostadora	toaster
trabajar	to work
trabajo	work
traducir	to translate
traer	to bring
traje	suit
traje de noche	evening gown
tranquilo	calm

transferencia	transfer
trapeador	mop
trapo	rag
tren	train
triste	sad
triturador	garbage disposal
tronco	trunk
tú	you
tubería	pipe
tubo	tube
último	last
un	a, an
uñas	nails
unir	to join
urgente	urgent
usar	to use
útil	useful
uva	grape
vaca	cow
vacaciones	vacation
vacío	empty
vacuno	beef
valla	fence
valle	valley
vapor	steam, vapor
varios	several
varón	male
vaso	glass

vecino	neighbor
vejiga	bladder
vela	candle
velocidad	speed
vena	vein
vendedor	salesman
vender	to sell
veneno	poison
venir	to come
ventaja	advantage
ventana	window
ventanilla	box office or ticket window
ventilador	fan
ver	to see
verano	summer
verdad	truth
verde	green
vergüenza	shame
vestido	dress
vestuarios	dressing room
viajar	to travel
viaje	journey, trip
viajero	traveler, passenger
vida	life
vidriera	stained-glass window
viejo	old
viento	wind

viernes	Friday
vino	wine
violeta	violet, purple
vista	sight
vivir	to live
volante	steering wheel
volar	to fly
volumen	volume
volver	to come back
vómito	vomit
votar	to vote
voz	voice
vuelo	flight
y	and
yarda	yard
yerno	son-in-law
yeso	plaster
yo	I
yogur	yogurt
zanahoria	carrot
zancudo (also *mosquito*)	mosquito
zapatera	shoe rack
zapatero	shoemaker, cobbler
zapatillas	slippers, sneakers
zapato	shoe
zapatos de deporte	running shoes
zapatos de tacón alto	high heels

The Most Useful
Spanish Words
English-to-Spanish
Alphabetical List

a, an	*un*
abdomen	*abdomen*
able	*capaz*
about	*acerca*
above	*encima*
accept	*aceptar*
accessories	*complementos*
access	*acceso*
according to	*según*
to accompany	*acompañar*
account, bill	*cuenta*
accountant	*contable, contador*
acid	*ácido*
across	*a través*
act	*acto*
action	*acción*
to add	*añadir*
addition	*suma*
address, direction	*dirección*
addressee	*destinatario*

adhesive tape	*cinta adhesiva*
adjustment	*ajuste*
advantage	*ventaja*
advertisement, announcement	*anuncio*
to advise	*aconsejar*
affectionate	*cariñoso*
after	*después, luego*
again	*de nuevo*
against	*contra*
age	*edad*
agent	*agente*
agreement	*acuerdo*
air	*aire*
airplane	*avión*
aisle	*pasillo*
alarm clock	*reloj de alarma*
allergy	*alergia*
all, everything	*todo*
almost	*casi*
alone	*solo*
also	*también*
although	*aunque*
always	*siempre*
among, between	*entre*
amusement	*diversión*
and	*y*

anesthesia	*anestesia*
angle	*ángulo*
angry	*enojado*
animal	*animal*
ankle	*tobillo*
to annoy	*molestar, fastidiar*
answer	*respuesta*
to answer	*responder*
ant	*hormiga*
antacid	*antiácido*
antihistamine	*antihistamínico*
any	*cualquiera*
apartment	*apartamento*
apparatus	*aparato*
to appear	*aparecer*
apple	*manzana*
appointment	*cita*
approach	*acercamiento, enfoque*
approval	*aprobación*
apricot	*albaricoque*
April	*abril*
arch	*arco*
architect	*arquitecto*
argument, discussion	*discusión*
arm	*brazo*
army	*ejército*

arrival	*llegada*
to arrive	*llegar*
art	*arte*
artichoke	*alcachofa*
article	*artículo*
artist	*artista*
ashtray	*cenicero*
to ask	*preguntar*
asparagus	*espárragos*
at, on, in	*en*
to attach	*adjuntar*
attack	*ataque*
attempt	*intento*
attention	*atención*
attraction	*atracción*
auburn	*caoba*
August	*agosto*
aunt	*tía*
authority	*autoridad*
automatic	*automático*
automobile	*automóvil*
avenue	*avenida*
avocado	*aguacate*
awake	*despierto*
baby	*bebé*
baby bottle	*biberón, mamadera*
baby-bottle nipple	*mamila*

baby food	*comida para bebé*
baby wipes	*toallitas húmedas*
back	*espalda*
bad	*malo*
bag	*bolsa*
baker	*panadero*
bakery	*panadería*
balance	*equilibrio*
balance	*saldo*
balcony	*balcón*
ball	*pelota*
ballpoint pen	*bolígrafo*
banana	*banana*
band	*banda, grupo*
bangs	*flequillo*
base	*base*
basket	*cesta*
bassinet	*moisés*
bath	*baño*
to bathe	*bañar*
bathtub	*bañera, tina*
battery	*pila*
to be	*estar, ser*
beach	*playa*
beans	*frijoles*
bear	*oso*
beard	*barba*

beauty cream	*crema de belleza*
beautiful	*bella, bello*
because	*porque*
bed	*cama*
bedroom	*alcoba, dormitorio*
bedspread	*colcha*
bee	*abeja*
beef	*carne de vaca, carne de res*
beetroot	*remolacha*
before	*antes*
behavior	*comportamiento*
behind	*atras, detrás*
to begin	*comenzar*
belief	*creencia*
to believe	*creer*
bell	*campana*
to belong	*pertenecer*
belt	*cinturón*
bench	*banco*
bent	*doblado*
beside	*al lado*
better	*mejor*
bicycle	*bicicleta*
bidet	*bidé*
big	*grande*
bill	*factura, cuenta*

bird	*pájaro*
birth	*nacimiento*
birthday	*cumpleaños*
a bit	*un poco*
bit	*trozo, pedazo*
bitter	*amargo*
black	*negro*
blackboard	*pizarra*
bladder	*vejiga*
blade	*cuchilla*
blanket	*cobija, manta*
bleach	*cloro*
blender	*batidora*
blind	*ciego*
block	*cuadra*
blond	*rubio*
blood	*sangre*
blouse	*blusa*
blow	*golpe*
blow dry	*alisado con secador*
blue	*azul*
board	*tabla*
boat	*barco*
body	*cuerpo*
boiled	*cocido, hervido*
boiling	*hervir*
bologna	*mortadela*

bone	*hueso*
book	*libro*
bookstore	*librería*
boot	*bota*
border	*frontera*
to be born	*nacer*
boss, chief	*jefe, patrón*
both	*ambos*
to bother	*molestar*
bottle	*botella*
bottle opener	*destapador*
bowl	*tazón*
box	*caja*
box office or ticket	
window	*ventanilla*
boy	*niño, muchacho*
boyfriend	*novio*
bra	*brasier, sostén*
bracelet	*pulsera*
brain	*cerebro*
brake	*freno*
branch	*rama*
brass	*latón*
bread	*pan*
to break	*romper*
breakfast	*desayuno*
breath	*aliento*

to breathe	*respirar*
brick	*ladrillo*
bridge	*puente*
bright	*brillante*
to bring	*traer*
broccoli	*brécol, brócoli*
broken	*roto*
broken bone	*hueso roto*
broom	*escoba*
brother	*hermano*
brother-in-law	*cuñado*
brown	*marrón*
browser	*navegador*
bruise	*moretón*
brunet, brunette	*moreno, morena*
brush	*cepillo*
Brussels sprouts	*coles de Bruselas*
bucket	*cubo*
budget	*presupuesto*
building	*edificio*
bulb	*bulbo*
bull	*toro*
bump	*bulto, choque, chichón*
burn	*quemadura*
to burn	*quemar*
burp	*eructar*

bus	*autobús*
business	*negocio*
businessman	*empresario*
busy	*ocupado*
but	*pero*
butcher's shop	*carnicería*
butter	*mantequilla*
button	*botón*
to buy, to shop	*comprar*
by	*por*
cabbage	*col, repollo*
cake	*pastel*
calf	*pantorrilla*
call	*llamada*
to call	*llamar*
calm	*tranquilo*
camera	*cámara*
can	*lata*
canary	*canario*
candle	*vela*
canvas	*lienzo*
car seat	*asiento de automovil*
card	*tarjeta*
carpenter	*carpintero*
carrot	*zanahoria*
to carry	*llevar*
cart	*carro*

carving fork	*tenedor de trinchar*
cash	*dinero en efectivo*
cashier	*caja, cajero*
castle	*castillo*
cat	*gato*
cauliflower	*coliflor*
to cause	*causar*
ceiling	*techo*
celery	*apio*
center	*centro*
centigrade	*centígrado*
centimeter	*centímetro*
century	*siglo*
cereal	*cereal*
certain	*cierto*
certified	*certificado*
chain	*cadena*
chair	*silla*
chalk	*tiza*
chance	*oportunidad*
change	*cambio*
to change	*cambiar*
charge	*cobro*
to charge	*cargar*
cheap	*barato*
check	*cheque, cuenta*
checking account	*cuenta corriente*

cheek	*mejilla*
cheese	*queso*
chemical	*químico*
cherry	*cereza*
chest, breast	*pecho*
chestnut	*castaño*
chickpeas	*garbanzos*
chicken	*pollo*
child	*niño, niña*
chill	*escalofrío*
chimney	*chimenea*
chin	*barbilla*
to choose	*escoger*
Christmas	*Navidad*
church	*iglesia*
cinnamon	*canela*
circle	*círculo*
citizen	*ciudadano*
city	*ciudad*
clam	*almeja*
to clarify	*aclarar*
classroom	*clase, salón*
clean	*limpio*
to clean	*limpiar*
client	*cliente*
climate	*clima*
clip	*clip*

clock	*reloj*
closet	*armario*
cloth	*tela*
cloth, duster	*paño*
clothes	*ropa*
clothesline	*tendedero*
clothes peg	*pinzas*
clothes rack	*perchero*
cloud	*nube*
cloudy	*nublado*
coal	*carbón*
coast	*costa*
coat	*abrigo*
coffee machine	*máquina de café*
coffee pot	*cafetera*
coffee spoon	*cucharita de café*
coffee table	*mesa de café*
coin	*moneda*
coincidence	*coincidencia*
cold	*frío, resfriado*
cold water	*agua fría*
cologne	*colonia*
color	*color*
colored clothes	*ropa de color*
colored pencils	*lápices de colores*
comb	*peine*
to come	*venir*

to come back	*volver*
comfort	*comodidad*
comfortable	*cómodo*
comforter	*edredón*
committee	*comité*
common	*común*
company	*compañía*
comparison	*comparación*
competition	*competencia, concurso*
to complain	*quejarse*
complaint	*queja*
complete	*completo*
to complete	*completar*
complex	*complejo*
computer	*computadora*
condition	*condición*
conditioner	*suavizante*
conference	*conferencia*
confused	*confundido*
congratulations	*felicidades*
connection	*conexión*
conscious	*consciente*
consulate	*consulado*
container	*envase, recipiente*
to continue	*continuar*
control	*control*

cook	*cocinero*
to cook	*cocinar*
cooked	*cocinado*
cookies	*galletas*
copper	*cobre*
copy	*copia*
to copy	*copiar*
cord	*cable*
cork	*corcho*
corkscrew	*sacacorchos*
corn	*maíz, elote*
corner	*esquina*
correct	*correcto*
cotton	*algodón*
cotton tips	*palitos de algodón*
couch	*sofá*
cough	*tos*
to cough	*toser*
cough syrup	*jarabe para la tos*
to count	*contar*
country	*país*
course	*curso*
cousin	*prima, primo*
to cover	*cubrir*
cow	*vaca*
crack	*grieta*

crackers	galletitas saladas
crane	grúa
to crash	chocar
crayons	ceras
crazy	loco
cream	crema
cream for insect bites	crema para picaduras
credit	crédito
credit card	tarjeta de crédito
crib	cuna
crime	crimen
cross	cruz
to cross	cruzar
crow	cuervo
cruel	cruel
to crush	aplastar
to cry	llorar
cucumber	pepino
cup	copa, taza
curler	rulo
curls	rizos
current	actual
curtain	cortina
curve	curva
cushion	almohada
custom	costumbre
customs	aduana

cut	*corte*
to cut	*cortar*
cycle	*ciclo*
daisy	*margarita*
to damage	*dañar*
dance	*baile*
to dance	*bailar*
danger	*peligro*
dangerous	*peligroso*
to dare	*atreverse*
dark	*oscuro*
database	*base de datos*
date	*fecha*
daughter	*hija*
daughter-in-law	*nuera*
day	*día*
dead	*muerto*
dear	*querido*
death	*muerte*
debt	*deuda*
to deceive	*engañar*
December	*diciembre*
to decide	*decidir*
decision	*decisión*
deep	*profundo*
degree	*grado*
delay	*retraso*

delicate	*delicado*
delighted	*encantado*
to deliver	*entregar*
to demand	*exigir*
dental floss	*hilo dental*
dentist	*dentista*
to deny	*negar*
deodorant	*desodorante*
department store	*almacén*
dependent	*dependiente*
depilation	*depilación*
deposit, tank	*depósito*
to deserve	*merecer*
design	*diseño*
desire	*deseo*
to desire	*desear*
desk	*pupitre, escritorio, mesa*
destination	*destino*
destruction	*destrucción*
detail	*detalle*
detergent	*detergente*
to develop	*desarrollar*
to develop film	*revelar*
development	*desarrollo*
diaper	*pañal*
diarrhea	*diarrea*

to die	*morir*
diesel	*gasoil*
different	*diferente*
difficult	*dificultad*
digestion	*digestión*
dining table	*mesa de comer*
dining room	*comedor*
dirty	*sucio*
to discover	*descubrir*
discovery	*descubrimiento*
disease	*enfermedad*
disgust	*asco*
dish, plate	*plato*
dishwasher	*lavaplatos*
dishwasher soap	*jabón lavavajillas*
display, screen	*pantalla*
distance	*distancia*
distribution	*distribución*
division	*división*
dizziness	*mareo*
to do, to make	*hacer*
doctor	*médico*
dog	*perro*
doll	*muñeca*
dollar	*dólar*
dolphin	*delfín*
donkey	*burro*

door	*puerta*
doorbell	*timbre*
double bed	*cama de matrimonio*
double room	*habitación doble*
to doubt	*dudar*
down	*abajo*
download	*descargar*
dozen	*docena*
drag	*arrastrar*
drain	*desagüe*
drawer	*cajón*
drawing	*dibujo*
dress	*vestido*
dressing room	*vestuarios*
dressing table	*tocador*
drill	*taladradora*
drink	*bebida*
to drink	*beber*
driver	*chófer*
driving	*manejar*
drop	*gota*
drunk	*borracho*
dry	*seco*
to dry	*secar*
dry cleaning	*limpieza en seco*
dryer	*secadora*
dust, powder	*polvo*

dustpan	*recogedor*
DVD player	*lector de DVD*
dye	*tinte, colorante*
eagle	*águila*
ear	*oído, oreja*
ear wax	*cerumen*
early	*temprano*
to earn	*ganar*
earring	*arete*
to eat	*comer*
earth, land, soil	*tierra*
east	*este*
easy	*fácil*
economist	*economista*
edge	*borde*
education	*educación*
effect	*efecto*
effort	*esfuerzo*
egg	*huevo*
eggplant	*berenjena*
elastic	*elástico*
elbow	*codo*
electrician	*electricista*
elephant	*elefante*
elevator	*elevador*
e-mail	*correo electrónico*
to embrace	*abrazar*

employee	*empleado*
employment	*empleo*
empty	*vacío*
end	*fin*
endives	*endivias*
engagement	*compromiso*
engine	*motor*
engineer	*ingeniero*
English	*inglés*
to enjoy, to have a good time	*disfrutar*
enough	*bastante, suficiente*
to enter	*entrar*
entrance	*entrada*
envelope	*sobre*
equal	*igual*
error	*error*
escalator	*escalera mecánica*
even	*incluso*
evening gown	*traje de noche*
event	*evento*
every, each	*cada*
everybody	*todos*
exam	*examen*
example	*ejemplo*
exchange	*cambio*
existence	*existencia*

exit	*salida*
expansion	*expansión*
expensive	*caro*
experience	*experiencia*
experiment	*experimento*
expert	*experto*
to explain	*explicar*
to explode	*explotar*
eye	*ojo*
eye drops	*colirio*
eyelash	*pestaña*
eyebrow	*ceja*
eyeglasses	*gafas*
eyelid	*párpado*
face	*rostro*
facial	*limpieza de cutis*
fact	*hecho*
factory	*fábrica*
to fail	*fallar*
faith	*fe*
fall	*caída*
fall	*otoño*
to fall	*caer*
false	*falso*
family	*familia*
famous	*famoso*
fan	*ventilador*

fantastic	*fantástico*
far	*lejos*
farm	*granja*
fashion	*moda*
fat	*gordo*
father	*padre*
father-in-law	*suegro*
faucet	*grifo, llave*
fax	*fax*
fear	*miedo*
feather	*pluma*
feather duster	*plumero*
February	*febrero*
feeble, weak	*débil*
feeling	*sentimiento*
female	*hembra*
fence	*valla*
fertile	*fértil*
fertilizer	*fertilizante*
fester	*supurar*
fever	*fiebre*
fever reducer	*antitérmico*
fiber	*fibra*
fiction	*ficción*
field	*campo*
fight	*lucha*
file	*lima*

filing cabinet	*archivador*
to fill	*llenar*
to find	*encontrar*
finger	*dedo*
to finish	*acabar*
fire	*fuego*
firma	*signature*
first	*primero*
fish	*pescado*
fish	*pez*
fishmonger's shop	*pescadería*
fist	*puño*
fitting room	*probador*
to fix	*arreglar*
fixed	*fijo*
flag	*bandera*
flame	*llama*
flight	*vuelo*
flight attendant	*azafata*
floor	*piso*
floor cleaner	*limpiador de suelos*
flower	*flor*
fly	*mosca*
to fly	*volar*
foam	*espuma*
fog	*niebla*
fold	*pliegue*

to fold	*doblar*
folder	*carpeta*
to follow	*seguir*
food	*comida*
foolish	*imprudente*
foot	*pie*
footrest	*reposapiés*
for	*para*
to forbid	*prohibir*
force	*fuerza*
forearm	*antebrazo*
forest	*bosque*
fork	*tenedor*
form	*forma*
forms	*formularios*
formula	*fórmula*
forward, ahead	*adelante*
fowl	*ave*
frame	*marco*
frying pan	*sartén*
freckle	*peca*
free	*gratis, libre*
freezer	*congelador*
French	*francés*
frequent	*frecuente*
fresh	*fresco*
friday	*viernes*

fried	*frito*
friend	*amigo*
friendship	*amistad*
frog	*rana*
from, of	*de*
front, forehead	*frente*
frozen	*congelado*
fruit	*fruta*
fuchsia	*fucsia*
fuel	*combustible*
full	*lleno*
furniture	*muebles*
future	*futuro*
game	*juego*
garbage	*basura*
garbage disposal	*triturador*
garden	*jardín*
garlic	*ajo*
gasoline	*gasolina*
general	*general*
to get, to obtain	*obtener*
to get up	*levantarse*
gift, present	*regalo*
girl	*niña, muchacha*
girlfriend	*novia*
giraffe	*jirafa*
to give	*dar*

glass	*cristal, vaso*
glass cleaner	*limpiador de cristales*
glove	*guante*
glove compartment	*guantera*
gloves	*guantes*
to go	*ir*
go to bed	*acostarse*
to go down	*bajar*
to go up	*subir*
goat	*cabra*
god	*dios*
gold	*oro*
goldfinch	*jilguero*
good	*bueno*
good-bye	*adiós*
government	*gobierno*
grain	*grano*
gram	*gramo*
granddaughter	*nieta*
grandfather	*abuelo*
grandmother	*abuela*
grandson	*nieto*
grape	*uva*
grapefruit	*toronja, pomelo*
grass	*hierba, pasto*
grated cheese	*queso rallado*
grater	*rallador*

grease cleaner	*limpiador de grasa*
great	*fantástico*
green	*verde*
green beans	*ejotes, judías verdes*
green pepper	*pimiento verde*
to greet	*saludar*
greeting	*saludo*
grey	*gris*
grief	*pena*
grilled	*a la plancha*
groceries	*provisiones, compra*
group	*grupo*
to grow	*crecer*
guard	*guardia*
guest	*huesped*
guide	*guía*
gun	*pistola*
gymnastics	*gimnasia*
hair	*cabello*
hairdryer	*secador de pelo*
hake	*merluza*
half	*mitad*
ham	*jamón*
hammer	*martillo*
hand	*mano*
handrail	*baranda*
hand wash	*lavar a mano*

handkerchief	*pañuelo*
handsome	*guapo*
hanger	*percha*
to happen	*ocurrir*
happy	*feliz*
harbor	*puerto*
hard	*duro*
harmony	*armonía*
hat	*sombrero*
to hate	*odiar*
to have	*tener*
to have lunch	*almorzar*
he	*él*
head	*cabeza*
headphones	*auriculares*
health	*salud*
healthy	*saludable*
heart	*corazón*
hearts of palm	*corazón de palmito*
heat	*calor*
heavy	*pesado*
height	*altura*
hello	*hola*
help	*ayuda*
to help	*ayudar*
hen	*gallina*
here	*aquí*

to hide	*esconder*
high heels	*zapatos de tacón alto*
highway	*autopista*
hip	*cadera*
history	*historia*
to hit	*pegar*
hole	*agujero*
hole punch	*perforadora*
hollow	*hueco*
homepage	*página principal*
hook	*gancho*
hope	*esperanza*
to hope	*esperar*
horn	*bocina*
horse	*caballo*
hose	*manga de riego, manguera*
hospital	*hospital*
hot water	*agua caliente*
hour	*hora*
house	*casa*
hug	*abrazo*
humor	*humor*
hunger	*hambre*
hurry	*prisa*
to hurry	*apresurarse*
I	*yo*

ice	*hielo*
ice cubes	*cubitos de hielo*
ice cream	*helado*
idea	*idea*
if	*si*
ill, sick	*enfermo*
immediately	*inmediatamente*
important	*importante*
impulse	*impulso*
to improve	*mejorar*
in front of	*delante de*
in love	*enamorado*
inch	*pulgada*
increase	*incrementar*
indicator	*indicador,*
	intermitente
industry	*industria*
infection	*infección*
inflammation	*inflamación*
injury	*herida, lesión*
ink	*tinta*
insect	*insecto*
to insert	*insertar*
inside	*dentro*
instrument	*instrumento*
insurance	*seguro*
to insure	*asegurar*

interest	*interés*
interest rate	*tipo de interés*
Internet	*Internet*
interval	*intervalo*
invention	*invento, invención*
iron	*hierro, plancha*
to iron	*planchar*
ironing board	*tabla de planchar*
irritation	*irritación*
island	*isla*
itching	*comezón, picazón*
jacket	*chaqueta*
jail	*cárcel*
January	*enero*
jaw	*mandíbula*
jelly	*gelatina*
jewel	*joya*
jewelry store	*joyería*
to join	*unir*
joke	*broma, chiste*
journalist	*periodista*
journey	*viaje*
judge	*juez*
July	*julio*
to jump	*saltar*
June	*junio*
to keep	*mantener*

kettle	*hervidor*
key, faucet	*llave*
keyboard	*teclado*
kick	*patada*
kidney	*riñon*
kilo	*kilo*
kilometer	*kilómetro*
kind	*tipo*
king	*rey*
kiss	*beso*
to kiss	*besar*
kitchen	*cocina*
kiwi	*kiwi*
knee	*rodilla*
knife	*cuchillo*
knot	*nudo*
to know	*conocer, saber*
knowledge	*conocimiento*
ladle	*cucharón*
lady	*dama*
lake	*lago*
lamb	*cordero*
lamp	*lámpara*
landscape	*paisaje*
language	*idioma, lenguaje*
last	*último*
to last	*durar*

last night	*anoche*
late, afternoon	*tarde*
to laugh	*reír*
law	*ley*
lawn mower	*máquina de cortar pasto*
lawyer	*abogado*
laxative	*laxante*
lead	*plomo*
leaf	*hoja*
learning	*aprendizaje*
leather	*cuero*
to leave	*salir*
left	*izquierda*
leg	*pierna*
to lend	*prestar*
lentils	*lentejas*
less	*menos*
lesson	*lección*
to let	*dejar*
letter	*carta*
lettuce	*lechuga*
level	*nivel*
library	*biblioteca*
lie	*mentira*
life	*vida*
to lift	*levantar*

light	*luz*
lightbulb	*bombilla*
like, as	*como*
limit	*límite*
line	*línea*
linen	*lino*
link	*enlace*
lion	*león*
lip protector	*protector de labios*
lips	*labios*
liquor	*licor*
liquid	*líquido*
list	*lista*
listen	*escucha*
to listen	*escuchar*
little, small	*pequeño*
to live	*vivir*
liver	*hígado*
living room	*salón*
loan	*préstamo*
lock	*cerrojo*
locker	*armario*
long	*largo*
to look	*mirar*
to lose	*perder*
loss	*pérdida*
loud	*ruidoso*

loudspeaker	*altavoz*
love	*amor*
luck	*suerte*
luggage	*equipaje*
lung	*pulmón*
luxury	*lujo*
machine	*máquina*
madam	*señora*
magazine	*revista*
mail	*correo*
to make love	*hacer el amor*
male	*varón*
mall	*centro comercial*
man	*hombre*
manager	*gerente*
mango	*mango*
manicure	*manicura*
map	*mapa*
March	*marzo*
margarine	*margarina*
mark	*marca*
marker	*rotulador, marcador*
market	*mercado*
maroon	*granate*
marriage	*matrimonio*
married	*casado*
mashed potatoes	*puré de papas*

mass	*misa*
mat	*alfombrilla, felpudo*
match	*cerilla, fósforo*
material	*material*
math	*matemáticas*
matter	*asunto*
mattress	*colchón*
May	*mayo*
may	*poder*
mayonnaise	*mayonesa*
mayor	*alcalde*
meal, food	*comida*
measure	*medida*
meat	*carne*
meatballs	*albóndigas*
medicine chest	*botiquín*
medicine, drug	*medicina*
medlar tree	*níspero*
meeting	*reunión*
meeting room	*sala de reuniones*
melon	*melón*
member	*miembro*
memory	*memoria*
menu	*carta, menú*
metal	*metal*
metallic	*metálico*
meter	*metro*

method	*método*
microwave	*microondas*
middle	*medio*
midnight	*medianoche*
mile	*milla*
millimeter	*milímetro*
military	*militar*
milk	*leche*
mind	*mente*
mine	*mina, mío*
minute	*minuto*
miracle	*milagro*
mirror	*espejo*
misfortune	*desgracia*
to miss	*extrañar*
mist	*neblina*
mixed	*mezclado*
moisturizing cream	*crema hidratante*
Monday	*lunes*
money	*dinero*
monkey	*mono*
month	*mes*
moon	*luna*
mop	*trapeador*
more	*más*
moreover	*además*
morning	*mañana*

mortgage	*hipoteca*
mosquito	*mosquito, zancudo*
mosquito net	*mosquitera*
mother	*madre*
mother-in-law	*suegra*
motion, move	*movimiento*
mountain	*montaña*
mouse	*ratón*
mouth	*boca*
mouthwash	*enjuague bucal*
to move	*mover*
movie	*película*
movie theater	*cine*
much, very	*mucho*
mug	*jarra*
muscles	*músculo*
museum	*museo*
mushrooms	*champiñones, hongos*
music	*música*
music equipment	*equipo de música*
mussel	*mejillón*
my	*mi, mis*
nail	*clavo*
nails	*uñas*
name	*nombre*
nap	*siesta*
napkin	*servilleta*

narrow	*estrecho*
nation	*nación*
natural	*natural*
nausea	*náusea*
navy blue	*azul marino*
near, close	*cerca*
necessary	*necesario*
neck	*cuello*
necklace	*collar*
nectarine	*nectarina*
need	*necesidad*
to need	*necesitar*
needle	*aguja*
neighbor	*vecino*
neighborhood	*barrio*
neither	*ni, tampoco*
nephew	*sobrino*
nerve	*nervio*
net, network	*red*
never	*nunca*
new	*nuevo*
news	*noticia*
newspaper	*periódico*
next	*siguiente*
nice	*simpático, amable*
niece	*sobrina*
night	*noche*

nightdress, nightgown	*camisón*
nightstand	*mesita de noche*
no, not	*no*
nobody	*nadie*
node	*ganglio, nódulo*
noise	*ruido*
nonsmoker	*no fumador*
none	*ninguno*
noon	*mediodía*
north	*norte*
nose	*nariz*
note	*nota*
notebook	*cuaderno*
nothing	*nada*
November	*noviembre*
now	*ahora*
number	*número*
numbness	*insensibilidad, entumecimiento*
nuts	*nueces*
oats	*avena*
object	*objeto*
to oblige	*obligar*
observation	*observación*
ocean	*océano*
October	*octubre*
odor	*olor*

to offer	*ofrecer*
office	*oficina*
oil	*aceite*
old	*viejo*
olive oil	*aceite de oliva*
onion	*cebolla*
only	*solamente*
open	*abierto*
operation	*operación*
opinion	*opinión*
opportunity	*oportunidad*
opposite	*opuesto*
or	*o*
orange	*anaranjado, naranja*
orange juice	*jugo de naranja*
order	*orden, ordenar*
oregano	*orégano*
organization	*organización*
ornament	*ornamento*
other	*otro*
ounce	*onza*
our	*nuestro*
outside	*fuera*
oven	*horno*
over	*encima*
overdone	*recocido*
owner	*dueño, propietario*

pacifier	*chupón*
package	*paquete*
page	*página*
pain	*dolor*
pain reliever	*analgésico*
paint, painting	*pintura*
to paint	*pintar*
pair	*par*
pajamas	*pijamas*
palace	*palacio*
pale	*pálido*
pan	*sartén*
pantry	*despensa*
pants	*pantalones*
papaya	*papaya*
paper	*papel*
paragraph	*párrafo*
parallel	*paralelo*
parcel	*paquete*
pardon	*perdón*
park	*parque*
to park	*aparcar, estacionar*
part	*parte*
party	*fiesta*
to pass	*pasar*
passenger	*pasajero, viajero*
passport	*pasaporte*

password	*contraseña, clave*
past	*pasado*
pasta	*pasta*
paste	*pasta*
to pay	*pagar*
payment	*pago*
pea	*guisante, arbeja*
peace	*paz*
peach	*durazno, melocotón*
peanut	*cacahuate, maní*
pedestrian	*peatón*
pedicure	*pedicura*
pee	*pis*
peephole	*mirilla*
pen	*pluma*
pencil	*lápiz*
people	*gente*
pepper (spice)	*pimienta*
perfume	*perfume*
perfumery	*perfumería*
perhaps	*quizás*
perm	*permanente*
permission	*permiso*
to permit	*permitir*
person	*persona*
petite sizes	*tallas pequeñas*
petunia	*petunia*

pharmacy	*farmacia*
photo	*foto*
photocopier	*fotocopiadora*
photocopy	*fotocopia*
phrase	*frase*
physical	*físico*
physician	*médico*
pick	*pico*
to pick up	*recoger*
picture	*cuadro*
piece	*pieza*
pig, pork	*cerdo*
pigeon	*paloma*
pill	*píldora*
pillowcase	*funda de almohada*
pillow	*almohada*
pineapple	*piña*
pink	*rosado*
pipe	*tubería*
pity	*pena*
place	*lugar, sitio*
plant	*planta*
plantain	*plátano*
plaster	*yeso*
plastic	*plástico*
plasticine	*plastilina*
to play	*jugar*

playpen	*parquecito infantil*
plaza	*plaza*
please	*por favor*
pleasure	*placer*
pliers	*tenazas*
plough	*arado*
plug	*tapón*
plum	*ciruela*
plumber	*fontanero*
plus sizes	*tallas grandes*
pocket	*bolsillo*
poetry	*poesía*
point	*punto*
poison	*veneno*
poker	*atizador*
police	*policía*
to polish	*pulir*
polite	*cortés*
political	*político*
poor	*pobre*
port	*puerto*
portrait	*retrato*
position	*posición*
possible	*posible*
postcard	*postal*
pot	*olla*
potato	*papa*

power	*poder*
to prepare	*preparar*
prescription	*receta*
present	*presente*
pretty	*bonito*
price	*precio*
priest	*cura*
print	*imprimir*
prison	*prisión*
private	*privado*
probable	*probable*
problem	*problema*
process	*proceso*
produce	*producir*
professor	*profesor*
profit	*ganancia, beneficio*
project	*proyecto*
promise	*promesa*
to promise	*prometer*
proof	*prueba*
property	*propiedad*
prose	*prosa*
to protect	*proteger*
to protest	*protestar*
public	*público*
pull	*estirar*
to pump	*bombear*

pumpkin	*calabaza*
punishment	*castigo*
pupils	*pupilas*
purple	*violeta*
purpose	*propósito*
pus	*pus*
to push	*empujar*
to put	*poner*
quality	*calidad*
queen	*reina*
question	*pregunta*
quick	*rápido*
quiet	*callado*
rabbit	*conejo*
radio	*radio*
rag	*trapo*
rail	*raíl*
railroad	*ferrocarril*
rain	*lluvia*
to rain	*llover*
raincoat	*impermeable*
raisin	*pasa*
rake	*rastrillo*
range	*rango*
raspberry	*frambuesa*
rat	*rata*
rate	*índice*

raw	*crudo, poco hecho*
ray	*rayo*
reaction	*reacción*
to read	*leer*
reading	*lectura*
ready	*listo*
rear mirror	*espejo retrovisor*
reason	*razón*
receipt	*recibo*
to receive	*recibir*
reception desk	*recepción*
recipe	*receta*
to recognize	*reconocer*
record	*registro, documento*
red	*rojo*
red-haired, redhead	*pelirrojo*
refrigerator	*refrigerador*
regime	*régimen*
to regret	*lamentar*
regular	*regular, normal*
to reject	*rechazar*
relationship	*relación*
relative	*pariente, familiar*
religion	*religión*
to remain	*permanecer*
remedy	*remedio*
to remember	*recordar*

remote	*remoto*
remote control	*control remoto*
to rent	*alquilar*
to repeat	*repetir*
representative	*representante*
to request	*solicitar*
reservation	*reserva, reservación*
to reserve	*reservar*
resident	*residente*
to respect	*respetar*
responsible	*responsable*
rest	*resto*
to rest	*descansar*
restroom	*cuarto de baño*
to return	*regresar*
to reveal	*revelar*
reward	*recompensa*
rhythm	*ritmo*
rice	*arroz*
right	*derecho*
ring	*anillo, hornillo*
to rinse	*enjuagar*
ripe	*maduro*
river	*río*
road	*camino, carretera*
roasted	*asado*
rod	*barra*

to roll	*rodar*
roof	*techo*
room	*cuarto, habitación*
root	*raíz*
rough	*áspero*
round	*redondo*
route	*ruta*
rub	*frotar*
rubber mat	*alfombrilla de hule*
rug	*alfombra*
rule	*regla*
to run	*correr*
running shoes	*zapatos de deporte*
sad	*triste*
safe	*seguro*
to sail	*navegar*
salesman	*vendedor*
salmon	*salmón*
salt	*sal*
same	*mismo*
sample	*muestra*
sand	*arena*
sandals	*sandalias*
sane	*cuerdo*
sanitary napkins	*toallas sanitarias, compresas*
sardine	*sardina*

satisfied	*satisfecho*
Saturday	*sábado*
sauce	*salsa*
sauna	*sauna*
save	*guardar*
savings account	*cuenta de ahorros*
saw	*sierra*
to say	*decir*
to say good-bye	*decir adiós*
scale	*balanza, báscula*
schedule	*horario*
school	*escuela*
science	*ciencia*
scissors	*tijeras*
screw	*tornillo*
to screw	*atornillar*
screwdriver	*destornillador*
sea	*mar*
search	*búsqueda*
season	*estación*
seat	*asiento*
seat belt	*cinturón de seguridad*
second	*segundo*
secret	*secreto*
secretary	*secretaria*
secretion	*secreción*
section	*sección*

security	*seguridad*
to see	*ver*
seed	*semilla*
to seem	*parecer*
selection	*selección*
to sell	*vender*
to send	*enviar*
sender	*remitente*
sentence	*frase*
to separate	*separar*
September	*septiembre*
serious	*serio*
to serve	*servir*
servant	*sirviente*
several	*varios*
to sew	*coser*
sex	*sexo*
shade	*sombra*
shame	*vergüenza*
shampoo	*champú*
shark	*tiburón*
shaver	*máquina de afeitar*
she	*ella*
sheep	*oveja*
sheet	*sábana*
shellfish	*marisco*
shelf	*estante*

shelves	*estantería*
shipment	*envío*
shirt	*camisa*
shoe	*zapato*
shoemaker, cobbler	*zapatero*
shoe rack	*zapatera*
shop	*tienda*
shop window	*escaparate*
shopping cart	*carrito*
short	*bajo, corto*
shorts	*pantalones cortos*
shoulder	*hombro*
shout	*grito*
to shout	*gritar*
shovel	*pala*
to show	*mostrar*
shower	*ducha, regadera*
to shower	*ducharse*
shower curtain	*cortina de baño*
shrimp	*camarón*
side	*lado*
sideburns	*patillas*
sight	*vista*
sign	*signo*
to sign	*firmar*
signature	*firma*
silk	*seda*

silver	*plata*
simple	*simple*
sin	*pecado*
to sing	*cantar*
single bed	*cama individual*
single room	*habitación simple*
sink	*lavabo, pileta, pila*
sir	*señor*
sister	*hermana*
sister-in-law	*cuñada*
to sit down	*sentarse*
size	*talla, tamaño*
skeleton	*esqueleto*
skimmer	*espumadera*
skin	*piel*
skirt	*falda*
sky	*cielo*
sky blue	*celeste*
sleep	*sueño*
to sleep	*dormir*
slippers	*zapatillas*
slowly	*despacio, lentamente*
smart	*listo*
to smell	*oler*
smile	*sonrisa*
to smile	*sonreír*
smoke	*humo*

to smoke	*fumar*
smoker	*fumador*
snack	*merienda*
snake	*serpiente*
sneeze	*estornudo*
to snore	*roncar*
snow	*nieve*
to snow	*nevar*
soap	*jabón, detergente*
soccer	*fútbol*
sock	*calcetín, media*
softener	*suavizante*
sole fish	*lenguado*
some	*alguno*
someone	*alguien*
son	*hijo*
song	*canción*
son-in-law	*yerno*
soon	*pronto*
sore throat	*dolor de garganta*
soup tureen	*sopera*
sour cream	*crema agria*
south	*sur*
soy sprouts	*brotes de soya*
space	*espacio*
Spanish	*español*
spare tire	*rueda de repuesto*

sparrow	*gorrión*
spatula	*espátula*
to speak	*hablar*
speakers	*bocinas*
speed	*velocidad*
to spend	*gastar*
spicy	*picoso, picante*
spider	*araña*
spinach	*espinaca*
spin-dry	*centrifugado*
sponge	*esponja*
spoon	*cuchara*
sport	*deporte*
sprain	*esguince*
spring	*primavera*
squirrel	*ardilla*
stain	*mancha*
stained-glass window	*vidriera*
staircase	*escalera*
stamp	*sello*
stapler	*grapadora*
staple remover	*quitagrapas*
star	*estrella*
station	*estaçion*
statue	*estatua*
to steal	*robar*
steam	*vapor*

steering wheel	*volante*
step	*escalón, paso*
still	*todavía*
stir-fried	*rehogado*
stitches	*puntos*
stocking	*media*
stomach	*estómago*
stone	*piedra*
to stop	*parar*
storm	*tormenta*
story, tale	*cuento*
stove	*estufa*
straight	*derecho*
strange	*extraño*
strawberry	*fresa*
street	*calle*
strike	*huelga*
string	*cordel*
stroll	*paseo*
strong	*fuerte*
student	*alumno, estudiante*
to study	*estudiar*
study desk	*mesa de estudio*
success	*éxito*
suddenly	*súbitamente*
sugar	*azúcar*
suit	*traje*

suitcase	*maleta*
summer	*verano*
sun	*sol*
Sunday	*domingo*
sunscreen	*filtro solar*
sunset	*puesta de sol*
supermarket	*supermercado*
to support	*apoyar*
surname	*apellido*
to swear	*jurar*
sweat	*sudor*
sweater	*sueter*
sweet	*dulce*
sweet potato	*camote*
swelling	*hinchazón*
to swim	*nadar*
swimming pool	*piscina, alberca*
Swiss chard	*acelga*
tablecloth	*mantel*
table	*mesa*
tablespoon	*cucharada*
tail	*cola*
tall	*alto*
to take advantage of	*aprovecharse*
to take away	*quitar*
to take care	*cuidar*
to take out	*sacar*

tampon	*tampón*
tangerine	*mandarina*
to taste	*probar*
tax	*impuesto*
to teach	*enseñar*
teacher	*maestro*
team	*equipo*
teapot	*tetera*
teaspoon	*cucharita de té*
teddy bear	*osito*
telephone	*teléfono*
television	*televisor*
temperature	*temperatura*
tendon	*tendón*
to thank	*agradecer*
thanks	*gracias*
that	*aquel, aquella*
the	*el, la, los, las*
theater	*teatro*
then	*entonces*
there	*allí*
there is	*hay*
they	*ellos, ellas*
thief	*ladrón*
thigh	*muslo*
thin	*delgado*
to think	*pensar*

thirst	*sed*
those	*aquellos*
throat	*garganta*
to throw	*lanzar, tirar*
thumb	*pulgar*
thumbtack	*chincheta*
Thursday	*jueves*
thus	*así*
ticket	*boleto, recibo*
tie	*corbata*
tiger	*tigre*
time	*tiempo*
tip	*propina*
tire	*rueda*
tired	*cansado*
to	*a*
toad	*sapo*
toaster	*tostadora*
tobacco	*tabaco*
today	*hoy*
toes	*dedos de los pies*
together	*juntos*
toilet	*inodoro*
toilet brush	*escobilla del inodoro*
toiletries	*cosas de aseo*
tomato	*tomate*
tomorrow	*mañana*

ton	*tonelada*
tongue	*lengua*
too much	*demasiado*
tooth	*diente*
toothbrush	*cepillo de dientes*
to touch	*tocar*
to tow	*remolcar*
toward	*hacia*
towel	*toalla*
tower	*torre*
town hall	*ayuntamiento*
toy	*juguete*
train	*tren*
trainer	*entrenador*
transfer	*transferencia*
to translate	*traducir*
to travel	*viajar*
tray	*bandeja*
treadmill	*cinta para correr*
tree	*árbol*
trip	*viaje*
truck	*camión*
trunk	*tronco*
to trust	*confiar*
truth	*verdad*
to try	*intentar*
T-shirt	*camiseta*

tube	*tubo*
Tuesday	*martes*
turkey	*pavo*
turnip	*nabo*
typical	*típico*
ugly	*feo*
umbrella	*paraguas*
umbrella stand	*paragüero*
uncle	*tío*
under	*debajo*
to understand	*comprender*
underwear	*ropa interior*
until	*hasta*
up	*arriba*
urgent	*urgente*
to use	*usar*
useful	*útil*
useless	*inútil*
user name	*nombre de usuario*
vacation	*vacaciones*
vacuum cleaner	*aspiradora*
valley	*valle*
vase	*florero*
vein	*vena*
village	*pueblo*
violet	*violeta*
voice	*voz*

volume	*volumen*
vomit	*vómito*
to vote	*votar*
waist	*cintura*
to wait	*esperar*
waiter	*camarero, mesero*
to wake up	*despertarse*
to walk	*caminar*
wall	*pared*
to want	*querer*
warm	*caliente*
to wash	*lavar*
washcloth	*toallita de baño*
washing machine	*lavadora*
wasp	*avispa*
wastepaper basket	*papelera*
water	*agua*
water colors	*acuarela*
watercress	*berro*
watering can	*regadera*
watermelon	*sandía*
wax	*cera*
we	*nosotros*
Web page	*página Web*
wedding	*boda*
Wednesday	*miércoles*
weed	*mala hierba*

week	*semana*
to weigh	*pesar*
weight	*peso*
weight room	*sala de pesas*
weights	*pesas*
welcome	*bienvenida*
west	*oeste*
to wet	*mojar*
whale	*ballena*
wheelbarrow	*carretilla*
when	*cuando*
where	*dónde*
while	*mientras*
white	*blanco*
white bread	*pan blanco*
white clothes	*ropa blanca*
whole wheat bread	*pan integral*
why	*por qué*
wide	*ancho*
wind	*viento*
window	*ventana*
windshield	*parabrisas*
windshield wipers	*limpiaparabrisas*
wine	*vino*
wine glass	*copa de vino*
winter	*invierno*
wire	*alambre*
withdrawal	*retiro*

without	*sin*
wolf	*lobo*
woman	*mujer*
wood	*leña, madera*
wool	*lana*
word	*palabra*
work	*tarea, trabajo*
to work	*trabajar*
world	*mundo*
to worry	*preocuparse*
worse	*peor*
to wrap	*envolver*
wrapping paper	*papel para regalo*
wrench	*llave inglesa*
to write	*escribir*
wrinkle	*arruga*
wrist	*muñeca*
yam	*ñame*
yard	*yarda*
yellow	*amarillo*
yes	*sí*
yesterday	*ayer*
yogurt	*yogur*
you	*tú*
young	*joven*
zipper	*cremallera*
zucchini	*calabacín, calabacita*

Day–to–Day Life

At Home —ᴍ— En la casa

HALL – *ENTRADA, ANTESALA*

chain	*cadena*
chair	*silla*
clothes rack	*perchero*
coat	*abrigo*
doorbell	*timbre*
handrail	*baranda*
key	*llave*
lock	*cerrojo*
mat	*alfombrilla, felpudo*
peephole	*mirilla*
picture	*cuadro*
raincoat	*impermeable*
screen	*mosquitera*
shoe rack	*zapatera*
stained-glass window	*vidriera*
staircase	*escalera*
step	*escalón*
umbrella stand	*paragüero*

— Things to Do —

come in	*entrar*
clean your feet	*limpiarse los pies*
take off your coat	*quitarse el abrigo*
take off your shoes	*quitarse los zapatos*
wait a minute	*esperar un momento*
open the door	*abrir la puerta*
close the door	*cerrar la puerta*
ring the bell	*tocar el timbre*
leave the mail	*dejar el correo*

— Useful Sentences —

Is there any mail for me?	*¿Hay correo para mí?*
You can hang your coat here.	*Puede colgar aquí su abrigo.*
You can leave your umbrella here.	*Puede dejar aquí su paraguas.*
Please, wait a minute.	*Espere un momento, por favor.*
Before opening the door you should look through the peephole.	*Mire por la mirilla antes de abrir la puerta.*

LIVING ROOM – *SALÓN, SALA*

ashtray	*cenicero*
book	*libro*

candle	*vela*
chimney	*chimenea*
clock	*reloj*
coffee table	*mesa de café*
couch	*sofá*
cup	*copa, taza*
curtain	*cortina*
dining table	*mesa de comer*
door	*puerta*
DVD player	*lector de DVD*
fan	*ventilador*
floor	*piso*
footrest	*reposapiés*
fork	*tenedor*
furniture	*muebles*
glass	*vaso*
headphones	*auriculares*
knife	*cuchillo*
lamp	*lámpara*
loudspeaker	*altavoz*
music equipment	*equipo de música*
napkin	*servilleta*
plant	*planta*
pillow	*almohada*
poker	*atizador*
radio	*radio*
remote control	*control remoto*

rug	*alfombra*
shelves	*estantería*
spoon	*cuchara*
tablecloth	*mantel*
television	*televisor*
toy	*juguete*
vase	*florero*
volume	*volumen*
window	*ventana*
wood	*leña*

— Things to Do —

sit down	*sentarse*
eat	*comer*
light the chimney	*encender la chimenea*
listen to music	*escuchar música*
read	*leer*
relax	*relajarse*
chat	*platicar*
have a party	*tener una fiesta*
be with the family	*estar con la familia*

— Useful Sentences —

Do you want something to drink?	*¿Quieres beber algo?*
It's time for dinner.	*Es hora de cenar.*
Would you like another serving?	*¿Te apetece repetir?*

The food is delicious.	*La comida está deliciosa.*
Please sit down.	*Por favor, siéntate.*
Please, make yourself comfortable.	*Por favor, ponte cómodo.*

—m—

BEDROOM – *ALCOBA, CUARTO*

bed	*cama*
bedspread	*colcha*
blanket	*cobija, manta*
closet	*armario*
comforter	*edredón*
drawer	*cajón*
dressing table	*tocador*
hanger	*percha*
lamp	*lámpara*
nightgown	*camisón*
nightstand	*mesita de noche*
pajamas	*pijamas*
pillow	*almohada*
pillowcase	*funda de almohada*
sheet	*sábana*
shelves	*estantería*
slippers	*zapatillas*
study desk	*mesa de estudio*

— Things to Do —

sleep	*dormir*
wake up	*levantarse*
get dressed	*vestirse*
read	*leer*
rest	*descansar*
study	*estudiar*

— Useful Sentences —

I am tired, I am going to bed.	*Estoy cansado, me voy a dormir.*
I am going to read in my room for a while.	*Me voy a leer un rato en mi cuarto.*
I have lots of clothes in my closet.	*Tengo mucha ropa en mi armario.*
I am going to my room to study.	*Voy a estudiar en mi cuarto.*

—∿—

BATHROOM – *CUARTO DE BAÑO*

baby wipes	*toallitas húmedas*
bathtub	*bañera, tina*
beauty cream	*crema de belleza*
bidet	*bidé*
brush	*cepillo*
closet	*armario*

cold water	*agua fría*
cologne	*colonia*
comb	*peine*
cotton tips	*palitos de algodón*
dental floss	*hilo dental*
deodorant	*desodorante*
faucet	*grifo, llave*
foam	*espuma*
hairdryer	*secador de pelo*
hot water	*agua caliente*
medicine chest	*botiquín*
mirror	*espejo*
moisturizing cream	*crema hidratante*
mouthwash	*enjuague bucal*
perfume	*perfume*
plug	*tapón*
rubber mat	*alfombrilla de hule*
sanitary napkins	*toallas sanitarias, compresas*
shampoo	*champú*
shaver	*máquina de afeitar*
shelf	*estante*
shower	*ducha, regadera*
shower curtain	*cortina de baño*
sink	*lavabo, pileta, pila*
soap	*jabón*
sponge	*esponja*
steam	*vapor*

tampon	*tampón*
toilet	*inodoro*
toothbrush	*cepillo de dientes*
towel	*toalla*
washcloth	*toallita de baño*
wastepaper basket	*papelera*

— Things to Do —

take a bath	*bañarse*
take a shower	*ducharse*
wash your face	*lavarse la cara*
brush your teeth	*cepillarse los dientes*
comb your hair	*peinarse*
go to the bathroom	*ir al baño*

— Useful Sentences —

I am going to take a bath.	*Voy a darme un baño.*
The water is cold.	*El agua está fría.*
Where is the toilet paper?	*¿Dónde está el papel higiénico?*
The clean towels are in the closet.	*Las toallas limpias están en el armario.*
The bathroom needs to be cleaned.	*Hay que limpiar el baño.*

KITCHEN – *COCINA*

blender	*batidora*
bottle opener	*destapador, abrebotellas*
bowl	*tazón*
carving fork	*tenedor de trinchar*
cloth	*paño*
coffee pot	*cafetera*
coffee spoon	*cucharita de café*
container	*envase, recipiente*
corkscrew	*sacacorchos*
dish, plate	*plato*
dishwasher	*lavaplatos*
dishwasher soap	*jabón lavavajillas*
fire	*fuego*
fork	*tenedor*
freezer	*congelador*
garbage	*basura*
garbage disposal	*triturador*
glass	*vaso, vidrio*
grater	*rallador*
groceries	*provisiones, compras*
ice cubes	*cubitos de hielo*
knife	*cuchillo*
ladle	*cucharón*
microwave	*microondas*
mug	*jarra*

oven	*horno*
pan	*sartén*
pantry	*despensa*
pot	*olla*
recipe	*receta*
refrigerator	*refrigerador*
sink	*pila*
skimmer	*espumadera*
slice	*pala*
spatula	*espátula*
stove	*estufa*
soup tureen	*sopera*
spoon	*cuchara*
teapot	*tetera*
teaspoon	*cucharita de té*
timer	*temporizador*
toaster	*tostadora*
tray	*bandeja*
wine glass	*copa de vino*

— Things to Do —

cook	*cocinar*
wash dishes	*lavar los platos*
eat	*comer*
clean	*limpiar*
have coffee	*tomar café*

— Useful Sentences —

I am cooking a delicious dish.	*Estoy cocinando un plato delicioso.*
Can you help me with the groceries?	*¿Me puedes ayudar con las compras?*
I am cleaning the pantry.	*Estoy limpiando la despensa.*
The oven is hot.	*El horno está caliente.*
The dirty dishes go in the dishwasher.	*Los platos sucios se colocan en el lavaplatos.*
Dinner will be ready very soon.	*La cena estará lista muy pronto.*

—∞—

LAUNDRY ROOM – *LAVANDERÍA*

bleach	*cloro*
clean	*limpio*
clothesline	*tendedero*
clothes peg	*pinzas*
colored clothes	*ropa de color*
cycle	*ciclo*
dirty	*sucio*
dryer	*secadora*
hand wash	*lavar a mano*
indicator	*indicador*

iron	*plancha*
ironing board	*tabla de planchar*
rinse	*enjuagar*
soap	*detergente*
softener	*suavizante*
spin-dry	*centrifugado*
string	*cordel*
temperature	*temperatura*
time	*tiempo*
washing machine	*lavadora*
white clothes	*ropa blanca*

— Things to Do —

wash	*lavar*
iron	*planchar*
discolor	*desteñir*
wrinkle	*arrugarse*
hang	*colgar*

— Useful Sentences —

These clothes lose color.	*Esta ropa se destiñe.*
I am going to hang the clothes.	*Voy a colgar la ropa.*
The clothes need to be ironed.	*Hay que planchar la ropa.*
These clothes need to be washed by hand.	*Esta ropa hay que lavarla a mano.*
This is a long washing cycle.	*Este ciclo de lavado es largo.*
The temperature is hot.	*La temperatura está caliente.*

—m—

CLEANING TOOLS AND SUPPLIES –
UTENSILIOS Y PRODUCTOS DE LIMPIEZA

bleach	*cloro*
broom	*escoba*
bucket	*cubo*
cloth, duster	*paño*
dust	*polvo*
dustpan	*recogedor*
feather duster	*plumero*
floor cleaner	*limpiador de suelos*
glass cleaner	*limpiador de cristales*
gloves	*guantes*
grease cleaner	*limpiador de grasa*
mop	*trapeador*
rag	*trapo*
toilet brush	*escobilla del inodoro*
vacuum cleaner	*aspiradora*

— Things to Do —

clean	*limpiar*
dust	*limpiar el polvo*
mop	*trapear*
sweep	*barrer*
vacuum	*aspirar*

— Useful Sentences —

I am dusting.	*Estoy limpiando el polvo.*
I have to vacuum.	*Tengo que pasar la aspiradora.*
The windows are dirty.	*Las ventanas están sucias.*
I am going to mop the kitchen floor.	*Voy a trapear el suelo de la cocina.*
After sweeping the floor you have to dust.	*Después de barrer hay que limpiar el polvo.*

GARDEN – JARDÍN

daisy	*margarita*
fence	*valla*
fertilizer	*fertilizante*
flower	*flor*
gloves	*guantes*
grass	*pasto*
hose	*manga de riego, manguera*
lawn mower	*máquina de cortar pasto*
leaf	*hoja*
petunia	*petunia*
pick	*pico*
rake	*rastrillo*

road	*camino*
shovel	*pala*
soil	*tierra*
stone	*piedra*
tree	*árbol*
trunk	*tronco*
violet	*violeta*
weed	*mala hierba*
wheelbarrow	*carretilla*

— Things to Do —

plant	*plantar*
water	*regar*
pull out	*arrancar*
cut	*cortar*
rake	*rastrillar*
prune	*podar*

— Useful Sentences —

The garden is full of leaves.	*El jardín está lleno de hojas.*
I am going to prune the trees.	*Voy a podar los árboles.*
I am planting petunias.	*Estoy plantando petunias.*
The plants need fertilizer.	*Las plantas necesitan fertilizante.*
We need to pull out the weeds.	*Tenemos que arrancar las malas hierbas.*

At the Office —∾— En la oficina

adhesive tape	*cinta adhesiva*
ballpoint pen	*bolígrafo*
CD	*CD*
chair	*silla*
clock	*reloj*
clip	*clip*
coffee machine	*máquina de café*
computer	*computadora*
copy	*copia*
cork	*corcho*
desk	*escritorio, mesa*
display	*pantalla*
drawer	*cajón*
e-mail	*correo electrónico*
fax	*fax*
filing cabinet	*archivador*
folder	*carpeta*
forms	*formularios*
hole punch	*perforadora*
Internet	*Internet*
keyboard	*teclado*
marker	*rotulador, marcador*
meeting room	*sala de reuniones*
office	*oficina*
paper	*papel*

password	*contraseña, clave*
pen	*pluma*
pencil	*lápiz*
photocopier	*fotocopiadora*
photocopy	*fotocopia*
scissors	*tijeras*
secretary	*secretaria*
stapler	*grapadora*
staple remover	*quitagrapas*
telephone	*teléfono*
thumbtack	*chincheta*
work	*trabajo*

— Things to Do —

work	*trabajar*
write	*escribir*
type	*teclear*
fill out	*llenar*
erase	*borrar*

— Useful Sentences —

I have a lot of work today.	*Hoy tengo mucho trabajo.*
I need to type a letter.	*Tengo que teclear una carta.*
You need to fill out these forms.	*Necesita llenar estos formularios.*
My computer is not working.	*Mi computadora no funciona.*

At School —∿— En la escuela

blackboard	*pizarra*
book	*libro*
chalk	*tiza*
classroom	*clase, salón*
colored pencils	*lápices de colores*
crayons	*ceras*
desk	*pupitre, escritorio*
exam	*examen*
experiment	*experimento*
ink	*tinta*
language	*lenguaje*
lesson	*lección*
math	*matemáticas*
notebook	*cuaderno*
paper	*papel*
pencil	*lápiz*
professor	*profesor*
reading	*lectura*
sciences	*ciencias*
student	*estudiante*
teacher	*maestro, maestra*
water colors	*acuarela*
work	*tarea*

— Things to Do —

learn	*aprender*
study	*estudiar*
read	*leer*
draw	*dibujar*
jugar	*play*

— Useful Sentences —

I have to do my homework.	*Tengo que hacer mi tarea.*
I like going to school.	*Me gusta ir a la escuela.*
My teacher is very nice.	*Mi maestra es muy simpática.*

Taking Care of Children
Cuidando de los niños

baby bottle	*biberón, mamadera*
baby food	*comida para bebé*
baby wipes	*toallitas húmedas*
bassinet	*moisés*
bath	*baño*
bottle nipple	*mamila*

burp	*eructar*
car seat	*asiento de automovil*
cereal	*cereal*
cream	*crema*
crib	*cuna*
diaper	*pañal*
formula	*fórmula*
mattress	*colchón*
nap	*siesta*
pacifier	*chupón*
pajamas	*pijamas*
pee	*pis*
playpen	*parquecito infantil*
sleep	*dormir*
cotton tips	*palitos de algodón*
teddy bear	*osito*
toy	*juguete*

— Things to Do —

play	*jugar*
change the diaper	*cambiar el pañal*
feed	*dar de comer*
sleep	*dormir*
cry	*llorar*

— Useful Sentences —

The baby has his bottle at noon.	*El bebé toma su mamadera a mediodía.*
He has a dirty diaper and needs to be changed.	*Tiene el pañal sucio, hay que cambiarlo.*
The baby wants to sleep.	*El bebé tiene sueño.*
He has to sleep on his back.	*Tiene que dormir boca arriba.*

Shopping —∾— De compras

bag	*bolsa*
bakery	*panadería*
butcher's shop	*carnicería*
cashier	*caja, cajero*
change	*cambio*
department store	*almacén*
fishmonger's shop	*pescadería*
gift, present	*regalo*
jewelry store	*joyería*
mall	*centro comercial*
money	*dinero*

perfumery	*perfumería*
pharmacy	*farmacia*
shipment	*envío*
shop	*tienda*
shop window	*escaparate*
supermarket	*supermercado*
wrapping paper	*papel para regalo*

—w—

AT THE SUPERMARKET
(see also "Foods" section) —

EN EL SUPERMERCADO
(ver también la sección "Alimentos")

aisle	*pasillo*
bag	*bolsa*
can	*lata*
container	*envase*
cooked	*cocinado*
freezer	*congelador*
fresh	*fresco*
frozen	*congelado*
fruit	*fruta*
meat	*carne*
paper	*papel*
plastic	*plástico*

scale   *báscula*
section   *sección*
shelf   *estante*
shopping cart   *carrito*

—⚍—

AT THE DEPARTMENT STORE –
EN EL ALMACÉN

accessories   *complementos*
clothes   *ropa*
elevator   *elevador, ascensor*
escalator   *escalera mecánica*
fitting room   *probador*
jewelry store   *joyería*
mirror   *espejo*
petite sizes   *tallas pequeñas*
plus sizes   *tallas grandes*
receipt   *recibo*
shoes   *zapatos*
size   *talla*
tax   *impuesto*

—⚍—

AT THE PHARMACY –
EN LA FARMACIA

antacid	*antiácido*
antihistamine	*antihistamínico*
cream for insect bites	*crema para picaduras*
cough syrup	*jarabe para la tos*
diarrhea	*diarrea*
eye drops	*colirio*
fever reducer	*antitérmico*
laxative	*laxante*
lip protector	*protector de labios*
medicine	*medicina*
pain reliever	*analgésico*
prescription	*receta*
sunscreen	*filtro solar*

—∾—

AT THE HARDWARE STORE –
EN LA FERRETERÍA

drill	*taladradora*
hammer	*martillo*
lightbulb	*bombilla*

nail	*clavo*
paint	*pintura*
plaster	*yeso*
pliers	*tenazas*
saw	*sierra*
screw	*tornillo*
screwdriver	*destornillador*
tube	*tubo*
wire	*alambre*
wood	*madera*
wrench	*llave inglesa*

— Things to Do —

exchange	*cambiar*
return	*regresar*
try on	*probar*

— Useful Sentences —

Can you wrap it for a present?	*¿Me lo puede envolver para regalo?*
Can I return it if it doesn't fit me?	*¿Puedo regresarlo si no me está bien?*
Can you give me a larger size, please?	*¿Me podría dar una talla más grande por favor?*
I would like to see some other items.	*Me gustaría ver otros modelos.*

At the Dry Cleaner/Laundromat
—m—
En la tintorería/lavandería

to dry	*secar*
dry cleaning	*limpieza en seco*
dryer	*secadora*
dye	*tinte*
to fold	*doblar*
iron	*plancha*
to pick up	*recoger*
ready	*listo*
stain	*mancha*
to wash	*lavar*
wrinkles	*arrugas*

— Things to Do —

iron	*planchar*
pick up	*recoger*
fold	*doblar*
wash	*lavar*
dry	*secar*

— Useful Sentences —

When can I pick it up?	*¿Cuándo puedo recogerlo?*
Could it be ready sooner? It's urgent.	*¿Podría estar listo antes? Es urgente.*

This suit needs to be dry cleaned.	*Este traje tiene que ser limpiado en seco.*
I want my shirts washed and ironed, please.	*Quiero mis camisas lavadas y planchadas, por favor.*
This rug is very delicate.	*Esta alfombra es muy delicada.*

At the Bank ~~ En el banco

balance	*saldo*
bill	*factura*
cashier	*cajero*
charge	*cobro*
check	*cheque*
checking account	*cuenta corriente*
deposit	*depósito*
interest rate	*tipo de interés*
loan	*préstamo*
money	*dinero*
mortgage	*hipoteca*
savings account	*cuenta de ahorros*
signature	*firma*
transfer	*transferencia*
withdrawal	*retiro*

— Things to Do —

open	*abrir*
withdraw	*retirar*
close	*cerrar*
pay	*pagar*

— Useful Sentences —

I want to know my balance, please.	*Quiero saber cuál es mi saldo, por favor.*
I want to open a checking account at your bank.	*Deseo abrir una cuenta corriente en su banco.*
What are your interest rates?	*¿Qué tipo de interés ofrecen?*
My stocks are down.	*Mis acciones han bajado.*
I paid a lot of bills this month.	*Este mes he pagado muchas facturas.*

At the Post Office
En la oficina de correos

addressee	*destinatario*
box	*caja*
certified	*certificado*
envelope	*sobre*

letter	*carta*
parcel	*paquete*
postcard	*postal*
receipt	*recibo*
regular	*regular*
sender	*remitente*
shipment	*envío*
stamp	*sello*
urgent	*urgente*

— Things to Do —

send	*enviar*
weight	*pesar*
receive	*recibir*
stamp	*sellar*
pick up	*recoger*
keep	*guardar*
certify	*certificar*

— Useful Sentences —

I want a stamp for this postcard, please.	*Quiero un sello para esta postal, por favor.*
I want to send it certified and urgent, please.	*Quiero enviarlo certificado y urgente, por favor.*
How much are these stamps?	*¿Cuánto valen estos sellos?*
Is this parcel too big?	*¿Es demasiado grande este paquete?*

Internet —m— Internet

access	*acceso*
attach	*adjuntar*
browser	*navegador*
computer	*computadora*
connection	*conexión*
database	*base de datos*
download	*descargar*
drag	*arrastrar*
e-mail	*correo electrónico*
homepage	*página principal*
Internet	*Internet*
link	*enlace*
mouse	*ratón*
network	*red*
password	*contraseña, clave*
save	*guardar*
search	*búsqueda*
speed	*velocidad*
time	*tiempo*
user name	*nombre de usuario*
Web page	*página Web*

— Things to Do —

send	*enviar*
look	*mirar*

check	*comprobar*
look up	*buscar*
find	*encontrar*
browse, surf	*navegar*
download	*descargar*
upload	*cargar*

— Useful Sentences —

I want to see if I have messages.	*Quiero ver si tengo mensajes.*
What browser can I use?	*¿Qué navegador puedo usar?*
I need to find something on the Internet.	*Necesito buscar algo en Internet.*
The connection speed is good.	*La velocidad de la conexión es buena.*
The connection was interrupted.	*Se interrumpió la conexión.*
I have to download a file.	*Tengo que descargar un archivo.*

At the Auto Shop
—⚏—
En el taller de autos

brake	*freno*
crane	*grúa*

diesel	*gasoil*
door	*puerta*
engine	*motor*
fuel	*combustible*
gasoline	*gasolina*
glove compartment	*guantera*
indicator	*intermitente*
oil	*aceite*
rear mirror	*espejo retrovisor*
roof	*techo*
seat	*asiento*
seat belt	*cinturón de seguridad*
spare tire	*rueda de repuesto*
steering wheel	*volante*
tank	*depósito*
tire	*rueda*
to tow	*remolcar*
window	*ventana*
windshield	*parabrisas*
windshield wipers	*limpiaparabrisas*

— Things to Do —

change	*cambiar*
repair	*reparar*
tow	*remolcar*
fill up	*llenar*
oil	*engrasar*

clean	*limpiar*
paint	*pintar*

— Useful Sentences —

I had a flat tire.	*Se me pinchó la llanta.*
I want to change the oil, please.	*Quiero cambiar el aceite, por favor.*
I need my car to be towed to a garage.	*Necesito remolcar mi auto a un garaje.*
Would you please fill up my tank?	*¿Puede llenar el depósito de mi auto, por favor?*

Traveling —⚬— De viaje

ON THE PLANE / TRAIN – *EN EL AVIÓN/TREN*

announcement	*anuncio*
citizen	*ciudadano*
connection	*conexión*
customs	*aduana*
delay	*retraso*
dizziness	*mareo*
drink	*bebida*
flight	*vuelo*
flight attendant	*azafata*

luggage	*equipaje*
meal	*comida*
passport	*pasaporte*
police	*policía*
resident	*residente*
restroom	*cuarto de baño*
screen	*pantalla*
seat	*asiento*
security	*seguridad*
suitcase	*maleta*
ticket	*boleto*

— Things to Do —

fly	*volar*
reserve	*reservar*
relax	*descansar*
buy	*comprar*
change	*cambiar*
wait	*esperar*

— Useful Sentences —

My flight has been delayed.	*Mi vuelo se ha retrasado.*
I want a window seat, please.	*Quiero un asiento al lado de la ventana, por favor.*
I need special assistance.	*Necesito ayuda especial.*
I want to change my flight.	*Quiero cambiar mi vuelo.*
I am traveling with children.	*Estoy viajando con niños.*

AT THE HOTEL – *EN EL HOTEL*

balcony	*balcón*
bathtub	*bañera, tina*
chair	*silla*
curtain	*cortina*
double bed	*cama de matrimonio*
double room	*habitación doble*
light	*luz*
pillow	*almohada*
reception desk	*recepción*
reservation	*reserva, reservación*
restroom	*cuarto de baño*
room	*cuarto, habitación*
shower	*ducha, regadera*
single bed	*cama individual*
single room	*habitación simple*
sink	*lavabo*
table	*mesa*
telephone	*teléfono*
television	*televisor*
toilet	*inodoro*
toiletries	*cosas de aseo*
towel	*toalla*
window	*ventana*

— Things to Do —

reserve	*reservar*
sleep	*dormir*
cancel	*cancelar*
clean	*limpiar*

— Useful Sentences —

Please hold my reservation; I will be arriving late.	*Por favor, guarde mi reservación; llegaré tarde.*
I would like a double room, please.	*Quiero una habitación doble, por favor.*
I have a reservation for three nights.	*He hecho una reserva por tres noches.*
Would you please wake me up at seven?	*¿Me podría despertar a las siete, por favor?*

At the Restaurant
En el restaurante

bill	*cuenta*
boiled	*cocido, hervido*
cash	*dinero en efectivo*
cook	*cocinero*

credit card	*tarjeta de crédito*
fried	*frito*
grilled	*a la plancha*
kitchen	*cocina*
liquor	*licor*
menu	*carta, menú*
napkin	*servilleta*
nonsmoker	*no fumador*
overdone	*muy hecho*
pepper	*pimienta*
raw	*poco hecho, crudo*
reservation	*reserva, reservación*
salt	*sal*
sauce	*salsa*
signature	*firma*
smoker	*fumador*
stir-fried	*rehogado*
sugar	*azúcar*
table	*mesa*
tablecloth	*mantel*
tip	*propina*
waiter	*mesero*
wine	*vino*

— Things to Do —

order	*ordenar*
reserve	*reservar*

pay	*pagar*
eat	*comer*

— Useful Sentences —

We have a reservation for four people.	*Tenemos reservada una mesa para cuatro personas.*
We are ready to order.	*Estamos listos para ordenar.*
Can I pay with a credit card?	*¿Puedo pagar con tarjeta de crédito?*
I like my meat well done, please.	*Me gusta la carne muy hecha, por favor.*

At the Beauty Salon
En el salón de belleza

bangs	*flequillo*
black	*negro*
blond	*rubio*
blow dry	*alisado con secador*
brush	*cepillo*
chestnut	*castaño*
comb	*peine*
conditioner	*suavizante*

curler	*rulo*
curls	*rizos*
depilation	*depilación*
dye	*tinte*
facial	*limpieza de cutis*
file	*lima*
hair	*cabello*
nails	*uñas*
manicure	*manicura*
perm	*permanente*
shampoo	*champú*
sideburns	*patillas*
pedicure	*pedicura*
redhead	*pelirrojo*

— Things to Do —

cut	*cortar*
comb	*peinar*
dye	*pintar*
file	*limar*

— Useful Sentences —

I want to cut my hair, please.	*Quiero cortarme el cabello, por favor.*
Please file my nails square.	*Lime las uñas cuadradas, por favor.*

I like this color for my nails.	*Me gusta este color para mis uñas.*
I would like a lighter color for my hair, please.	*Quiero un tono de tinte más claro para mi cabello, por favor.*

At the Gym —⌇— En el gimnasio

bicycle	*bicicleta*
dressing room	*vestuarios*
gymnastics	*gimnasia*
locker	*armario*
running shoes	*zapatos de deporte*
sauna	*sauna*
schedule	*horario*
shower	*ducha, regadera*
sweat	*sudor*
swimming pool	*piscina, alberca*
towel	*toalla*
treadmill	*cinta para correr*
trainer	*entrenador*
weight room	*sala de pesas*
weights	*pesas*

— Things to Do —

run	*correr*
swim	*nadar*
sweat	*sudar*
lift	*levantar*
jump	*saltar*

— Useful Sentences —

What is the gym's schedule?	*¿Cuál es el horario del gimnasio?*
Can I hire a trainer?	*¿Puedo contratar a un entrenador?*
How much is it per month?	*¿Cuánto vale al mes?*
At what time does the pool open?	*¿A qué hora está abierta la piscina?*

At the Doctor's Office
(see also "Parts of the Body")

—⚊—

En la oficina del doctor
(ver también "Partes del cuerpo")

allergy	*alergia*
anesthesia	*anestesia*

blood	*sangre*
broken bone	*hueso roto*
bruise	*moretón*
bump	*bulto*
chill	*escalofrío*
cold	*resfriado*
cut	*corte*
fester	*supurar*
fever	*fiebre*
infection	*infección*
inflamation	*inflamación*
injury	*herida, lesión*
irritation	*irritación*
itching	*comezón, picazón*
nausea	*náusea*
node	*ganglio*
numbness	*insensibilidad, entumecimiento*
pus	*pus*
secretion	*secreción*
sneeze	*estornudo*
sprain	*esguince*
sore throat	*dolor de garganta*
stitches	*puntos*
swelling	*hinchazón*
vomit	*vómito*

— Things to Do —

show	*mostrar*
examine	*examinar*
explain	*explicar*
hurt	*doler*
clean	*limpiar*
anesthesize	anestesiar
desinfect	*desinfectar*
sew	*coser*
put in plaster	*escayolar*
bandage	*vendar*
operate	*operar*

— Useful Sentences —

I don't feel good.	*No me siento bien.*
I have a fever.	*Tengo fiebre.*
It hurts here.	*Me duele aquí.*
I think my bone is broken.	*Creo que mi hueso está roto.*
The wound is infected.	*La herida está infectada.*
This area is very swollen.	*Este área está muy hinchada.*
Will I need stitches?	*¿Necesitaré puntos?*
Will I need surgery?	*¿Necesitaré cirugía?*
I am insured.	*Estoy asegurado.*
You can call my insurance company at this number.	*Puede llamar a mi seguro a este número.*

Romance —∞— Romance

boyfriend	*novio*
engagement	*compromiso*
girlfriend	*novia*
hug	*abrazo*
kiss	*beso*
love	*amor*
make love	*hacer el amor*
marriage	*matrimonio*
ring	*anillo*
sex	*sexo*
stroll	*paseo*
sunset	*puesta de sol*
wedding	*boda*

— Things to Do —

love	*amar*
stroll	*pasear*
kiss	*besar*
phone	*telefonear*

— Useful Sentences —

I like you very much.	*Tú me gustas mucho.*
I would like you to be my girl-friend.	*Me gustaría que fueras mi novia.*
Would you give me your phone number?	*¿Me darías tu número de teléfono?*
I love you.	*Te amo.*

Vocabulary Lists

Foods – *Alimentos*

apple	*manzana*
apricot	*albaricoque*
artichoke	*alcachofa*
asparagus	*espárragos*
avocado	*aguacate*
banana	*banana*
beans	*frijoles*
beef	*carne de vaca, carne de res*
beetroot	*remolacha*
bologna	*mortadela*
bread	*pan*
broccoli	*brécol, brócoli*
Brussels sprouts	*coles de Bruselas*
butter	*mantequilla*
cabbage	*col, repollo*
cake	*pastel*
carrot	*zanahoria*
cauliflower	*coliflor*
celery	*apio*
cereal	*cereal*
cheese	*queso*
cherry	*cereza*
chickpeas	*garbanzos*
chicken	*pollo*
cinnamon	*canela*

clam	*almeja*
cookies	*galletas*
corn	*maíz, elote*
crackers	*galletitas saladas*
cucumber	*pepino*
egg	*huevo*
eggplant	*berenjena*
endives	*endivias*
fish	*pescado*
garlic	*ajo*
grape	*uva*
grapefruit	*toronja, pomelo*
grated cheese	*queso rallado*
green beans	*ejotes, judías verdes*
green pepper	*pimiento verde*
hake	*merluza*
ham	*jamón*
hearts of palm	*corazón de palmito*
kiwi	*kiwi*
lamb	*cordero*
lentils	*lentejas*
lettuce	*lechuga*
mango	*mango*
margarine	*margarina*
mashed potatoes	*puré de papas*
mayonnaise	*mayonesa*
meat	*carne*

meatballs	*albóndigas*
medlar	*níspero*
melon	*melón*
milk	*leche*
mushrooms	*champiñones, hongos*
mussel	*mejillón*
nectarine	*nectarina*
nuts	*nueces*
oats	*avena*
olive oil	*aceite de oliva*
orange	*naranja*
orange juice	*jugo de naranja*
oregano	*orégano*
onion	*cebolla*
papaya	*papaya*
pea	*guisante, arbeja*
peach	*durazno, melocotón*
peanut	*cacahuate, maní*
pepper	*pimienta, pimiento*
pineapple	*piña*
plum	*ciruela*
potato	*papa*
pork	*cerdo*
pumpkin	*calabaza*
raisin	*pasa*
raspberry	*frambuesa*
rice	*arroz*

salmon	*salmón*
sardine	*sardina*
shellfish	*marisco*
shrimp	*camarón*
sole fish	*lenguado*
sour cream	*crema agria*
soy sprouts	*brotes de soya*
spinach	*espinaca*
strawberry	*fresa*
sugar	*azúcar*
Swiss chard	*acelga*
tangerine	*mandarina*
tomato	*tomate*
turkey	*pavo*
turnip	*nabo*
watercress	*berro*
watermelon	*sandía*
white bread	*pan blanco*
whole wheat bread	*pan integral*
yam	*ñame*
yogurt	*yogur*
zucchini	*calabacita*

COLORS – *COLORES*

black	*negro*
blue	*azul*

brown	*marrón*
fuchsia	*fucsia*
green	*verde*
grey	*gris*
maroon	*granate*
navy blue	*azul marino*
orange	*anaranjado*
pink	*rosado*
purple	*violeta*
red	*rojo*
sky blue	*celeste*
white	*blanco*
yellow	*amarillo*

Hair Colors – *Colores del cabello*

auburn	*caoba*
blond	*rubio*
blonde	*rubia*
brunet	*moreno*
brunette	*morena*
chestnut	*castaño*
red	*pelirrojo*

Eye Colors – *Colores de ojos*

black	*negro*
blue	*azul*
brown	*café*

green	*verde*
grey	*gris*
hazel	*miel*

NUMBERS – *NÚMEROS*

1	one	*uno*
2	two	*dos*
3	three	*tres*
4	four	*cuatro*
5	five	*cinco*
6	six	*seis*
7	seven	*siete*
8	eight	*ocho*
9	nine	*nueve*
10	ten	*diez*
11	eleven	*once*
12	twelve	*doce*
13	thirteen	*trece*
14	fourteen	*catorce*
15	fifteen	*quince*
16	sixteen	*dieciséis*
17	seventeen	*diecisiete*
18	eighteen	*dieciocho*
19	nineteen	*diecinueve*
20	twenty	*veinte*
21	twenty-one	*veintiuno*

22	twenty-two	*veintidós*
23	twenty-three	*veintitres*
24	twenty-four	*veinticuatro*
25	twenty-five	*veinticinco*
26	twenty-six	*veintiséis*
27	twenty-seven	*veintisiete*
28	twenty-eight	*veintiocho*
29	twenty-nine	*veintinueve*
30	thirty	*treinta*
100	one hundred	*cien*
1000	one thousand	*mil*
100,000	one hundred thousand	*cien mil*
1,000,000	one million	*un millón*

Seasons – *Estaciones*

spring	*primavera*
summer	*verano*
fall	*otoño*
winter	*invierno*

Months of the Year – *Meses del año*

January	*enero*
February	*febrero*
March	*marzo*

April	*abril*
May	*mayo*
June	*junio*
July	*julio*
August	*agosto*
September	*septiembre*
October	*octubre*
November	*noviembre*
December	*diciembre*

Days of the Week – *Días de la semana*

Monday	*lunes*
Tuesday	*martes*
Wednesday	*miércoles*
Thursday	*jueves*
Friday	*viernes*
Saturday	*sábado*
Sunday	*domingo*

Hours of the Day – *Horas del día*

noon	*mediodía*
12:00 P.M.	*las doce del mediodía*
1:00 P.M.	*la una de la tarde*
2:00 P.M.	*las dos de la tarde*
3:00 P.M.	*las tres de la tarde*
4:00 P.M.	*las cuatro de la tarde*

5:00 P.M.	*las cinco de la tarde*
6:00 P.M.	*las seis de la tarde*
7:00 P.M.	*las siete de la tarde*
8:00 P.M.	*las ocho de la noche*
9:00 P.M.	*las nueve de la noche*
10:00 P.M.	*las diez de la noche*
11:00 P.M.	*las once de la noche*
12:00 A.M.	*las doce de la noche*
midnight	*medianoche*
1:00 A.M.	*la una de la madrugada*
2:00 A.M.	*las dos de la madrugada*
3:00 A.M.	*las tres de la madrugada*
4:00 A.M.	*las cuatro de la madrugada*
5:00 A.M.	*las cinco de la mañana*
6:00 A.M.	*las seis de la mañana*
7:00 A.M.	*las siete de la mañana*
8:00 A.M.	*las ocho de la mañana*
9:00 A.M.	*las nueve de la mañana*
10:00 A.M.	*las diez de la mañana*
11:00 A.M.	*las once de la mañana*

MEASUREMENTS – *MEDIDAS*

centigrade	*centígrado*
centimeter	*centímetro (cm.)*
degree	*grado*
foot	*pie*
gram	*gramo (gr.)*

inch   *pulgada*

kilo   *kilo (kg.)*

kilometer   *kilómetro (km.)*

meter   *metro (m.)*

millimeter   *milímetro (mm.)*

ton   *tonelada*

yard   *yarda*

SITUATION – *SITUACIÓN*

beside   *al lado*

down   *abajo*

east   *este*

left   *izquierda*

north   *norte*

right   *derecha*

south   *sur*

straight   *derecho*

up   *arriba*

west   *oeste*

PARTS OF THE BODY – *PARTES DEL CUERPO*

abdomen   *abdomen*

ankle   *tobillo*

arm   *brazo*

back   *espalda*

bladder   *vejiga*

blood   *sangre*

bone	*hueso*
brain	*cerebro*
calf	*pantorrilla*
cheek	*mejilla*
chest, breast	*pecho*
chin	*barbilla*
ear	*oído, oreja*
ear wax	*cerumen*
elbow	*codo*
eye	*ojo*
eyebrow	*ceja*
eyelashes	*pestañas*
eyelid	*párpado*
finger	*dedo*
forearm	*antebrazo*
forehead	*frente*
fist	*puño*
freckle	*peca*
hair	*cabello*
hip	*cadera*
head	*cabeza*
heart	*corazón*
jaw	*mandíbula*
kidney	*riñon*
knee	*rodilla*
leg	*pierna*
lips	*labios*

liver	*hígado*
lung	*pulmón*
mouth	*boca*
muscle	*músculo*
nails	*uñas*
neck	*cuello*
nose	*nariz*
pupils	*pupilas*
shoulder	*hombro*
skeleton	*esqueleto*
skin	*piel*
stomach	*estómago*
tendon	*tendón*
thigh	*muslo*
throat	*garganta*
thumb	*pulgar*
toes	*dedos de los pies*
tooth	*diente*
tongue	*lengua*
vein	*vena*
waist	*cintura*
wrist	*muñeca*

CLOTHES – *ROPA*

blouse	*blusa*
bra	*brasier, sostén*
button	*botón*

coat	*abrigo*
dress	*vestido*
evening gown	*traje de noche*
high heels	*zapatos de tacón alto*
jacket	*chaqueta*
pants	*pantalon*
running shoes	*zapatos de deporte*
sandals	*sandalias*
shirt	*camisa*
shoe	*zapato*
shorts	*pantalones cortos*
skirt	*falda*
slippers	*zapatillas*
socks	*calcetines, medias*
sweater	*sueter*
tie	*corbata*
T-shirt	*camiseta*
underwear	*ropa interior*
zipper	*cremallera*

RELATIVES – *FAMILIARES*

aunt	*tía*
brother	*hermano*
brother-in-law	*cuñado*
cousin	*prima, primo*
daughter	*hija*
daughter-in-law	*nuera*

father	*padre*
father-in-law	*suegro*
granddaughter	*nieta*
grandfather	*abuelo*
grandmother	*abuela*
grandson	*nieto*
mother	*madre*
mother-in-law	*suegra*
nephew	*sobrino*
niece	*sobrina*
sister	*hermana*
sister-in-law	*cuñada*
son	*hijo*
son-in-law	*yerno*
uncle	*tío*

PROFESSIONS – *PROFESIONES*

accountant	*contable, contador*
architect	*arquitecto*
baker	*panadero*
carpenter	*carpintero*
dentist	*dentista*
doctor	*médico*
economist	*economista*
electrician	*electricista*
engineer	*ingeniero*
journalist	*periodista*

lawyer	*abogado*
plumber	*fontanero*
salesman	*vendedor*
teacher	*maestro*

ANIMALS AND INSECTS – *ANIMALES E INSECTOS*

ant	*hormiga*
bear	*oso*
bee	*abeja*
bird	*pájaro*
canary	*canario*
cat	*gato*
chicken	*pollo*
cow	*vaca*
crow	*cuervo*
dog	*perro*
dolphin	*delfín*
donkey	*burro*
eagle	*águila*
elephant	*elefante*
fish	*pescado, pez*
fly	*mosca*
frog	*rana*
giraffe	*jirafa*
goat	*cabra*
goldfinch	*jilguero*
hen	*gallina*

horse	*caballo*
insect	*insecto*
lion	*león*
monkey	*mono*
mosquito	*mosquito, zancudo*
mouse	*ratón*
pig	*cerdo*
pigeon	*paloma*
rabbit	*conejo*
rat	*rata*
shark	*tiburón*
sheep	*oveja*
snake	*serpiente*
sparrow	*gorrión*
spider	*araña*
squirrel	*ardilla*
tiger	*tigre*
toad	*sapo*
wasp	*avispa*
whale	*ballena*
wolf	*lobo*